The Best Little Girl in the World

STEVEN LEVENKRON

WARNER BOOKS

A Warner Communications Company

WARNER BOOKS EDITION

Copyright © 1978 by Steven Levenkron
All rights reserved.

This Warner Books Edition is published by
arrangement with Contemporary Books, Inc.,
180 North Michigan Avenue,
Chicago, Illinois 60601

Cover design by Gene Light
Cover photos by Bill Cadge

Warner Books, Inc.
666 Fifth Avenue
New York, N.Y. 10103

A Warner Communications Company

Printed in the United States of America

First Warner Books Printing: September, 1979

Reissued: May, 1981

20   19   18   17

She was a five-foot-four, ninety-eight-pound monster!

That's how Kessa saw herself, at any rate. She began tearing out the photographs of the thinnest models from her fashion magazine. *Soon I'll be thinner than all of you,* she swore to herself. *And then, I'll be the winner. The thinner is the winner.* She felt a contraction in her stomach, almost as if it were echoing her words, but she would not be intimidated by hunger pangs, despite the fact that it was two o'clock and she had eaten nothing so far today but half a grapefruit. *The thinner is the winner* she repeated, and smiled menacingly at the models, who grinned back at her in vacant pride at their own appearance.

Also by
Steven Levenkron

*The Best Little Girl
In The World*

*Treating And Overcoming
Anorexia Nervosa*

Kessa

For my wife Abby
and my daughters Rachel and Gabrielle

Fat and Skinny had a race
All around the pillow case.
Fat fell down and broke her face.
Skinny said, "Ha-ha,
I won the race."

1

At the barre the girls moved and stretched, pointed and arched in time to Madame's precise cadence. One, two, three, four . . .

I must be perfect, Francesca thought. She compared her own leg to the outstretched limb of the next girl and straightened her knee. "Five, six, seven, eight . . ." Madame continued to count, her pointer echoing the staccato beat. Francesca checked her leg against the girl on the other side. Straighter. The pleasure in her triumph dulled the pain behind her knee. Surely Madame would notice the perfection of her movements.

The studio was lined with mirrors. No matter where Francesca looked she could see legs stretching, arms arching, torsos bending, backs straightened in time to Madame's constantly demanding beat. In the mirror a black leotard, taut and slim and straight, caught Francesca's attention. She was perfect. Not an awkward gesture. Not an extra ounce of flesh. The figure was pure movement, all energy and strength for the dance.

Francesca turned from the girl's image to her own. Her thighs were grotesque bulges under the leg warmers. Above them her buttocks protruded

9

offensively. Her torso seemed to be all flab. Her breasts hung uselessly, obscuring the straight line that should have risen above her ribs. She was fat. Worse than that, she was a monster. A five-foot-four, ninety-eight-pound monster.

"One, two," Madame continued to count, and as she passed Francesca the staccato beat came out "well done." Had Francesca heard correctly? And if she had, were the words directed at her? The leg on her right reached higher. The girl on her left was slimmer and straighter. Francesca had to know. Had the words been said? Had they been meant for her? She wouldn't leave the studio until she found out.

When class was over Francesca stayed at the barre pretending to practice a last exercise until the handful of girls who normally clustered around Madame after each class had drifted off to change. She was not looking at the teacher but was acutely aware of her presence. Madame was gathering up her things. Soon she would be out of the room, and Francesca would never know. But how did she dare ask? The words echoed in her head foolishly. "Did you mean me when you said well done?" Impossible. "How was I today?" Sophomoric. A true dancer knew how she had performed. "Am I getting any better?" Worse than sophomoric. Babyish. And then, as if God or Madame or someone had answered her prayers, the teacher was standing beside her. Her dark reflection in the mirror next to Francesca's own blond one dazzled her. All the light that filtered in through the high windows seemed concentrated in the teacher's proud, bright eyes. Her body was straight and thin and firm. Without realizing it, Francesca drew her small slender frame up in imitation of the woman.

"A good class, Francesca. You're showing progress." The tones were as clipped and precise as her movements. "Now stay slim—perhaps even a pound less here." She touched Francesca's rear lightly. "And firm up." She patted the girl's stomach. "Slim and firm. It isn't enough to make you a dancer, but without it you'll never be a dancer." The words echoed in Francesca's head as she stared into the mirror at the woman's receding reflection. *Slim, firm, slim, firm.* They made a rhythm of their own. Like the *well done, well done* the teacher had thrown out during class.

Francesca had felt tired, but now she began to exercise again in time to the chant. She counted *slim, firm, slim, firm* to herself as Madame did the more conventional cadences. As she moved she observed herself closely in the mirror, still feeling where the teacher had touched her. It was as if her buttocks and stomach burned with the stinging rebuke. In the mirror her body seemed to swell and sag with every movement. She was worse than grotesque. There were no words for the slovenliness of Francesca's body, no words for the failure that was Francesca.

The idea came to her with a flash of excitement. Francesca was fat. Francesca was dead. She quickened her movements. *One, two, slim, firm, three, four, well, done,* and then, as if it came from the beat itself, the new girl was born, *Kes-sa, Kes-sa.* It matched the beat of Madame's stick. Better than that, it matched the beat of Madame herself. *Kes-sa, Ma-dame, Kes-sa, Ma-dame.* The name was brief, firm, and hard, just as Kessa would be. The name was born. The body would follow. The useless flesh and layers of revolting fat would fall away, and like her model, Madame, she would be pure strength and energy and movement. Fat Francesca was dead, had died giving birth to perfect Kessa.

The changing room was a bedlam of practice clothes and dance shoes and young, high-fluted voices. Giggles, shouts, whispered confidences. "I don't think she's all that good." This last, murmured just as she passed, Kessa was sure was said about her. For a moment she felt like crying. Then she remembered Madame. What did the opinion of some silly girl her own age matter against the superior wisdom.

"Hey, Francesca," the blond girl who had whispered the dire comment shouted, "we're going to Charlie's Soup Burg for something to eat. Want to come along?"

Reactions raced through Kessa's mind. They didn't mean me after all. They couldn't have meant me or they wouldn't ask me along. But of course they meant me, and now they're trying to make it up. Or they want me to come along so they can laugh at me. *Kes-sa, Kes-sa.* Her clenched fists beat in time against her thighs. But how could Kessa live if Francesca kept stuffing her with hamburgers and French fries and disgusting, fattening food?

"I'm not hungry," she lied, and turned her back on the girls to change. The battle had been joined, the first skirmish won.

Her step as she walked along Fifty-second Street was light. *Kes-sa, Kes-sa, Kes-sa.* She moved in time to her own rhythm now. She felt light and full of energy. How silly people were to eat. They thought they needed food for energy, but they didn't. Energy came from will, from self-control. Kessa, almost skipping now in time to her new name, was proof of that. She stopped at the corner waiting for the light to change. From the newsstands a dozen models smiled up at her from a dozen magazine covers, smiled in thin-faced, high-cheekboned agreement to Kessa's new discovery. They knew the secret too. They knew thin was good, thin was strong; thin was safe.

The windows were open, and the breeze from the park sent the curtains billowing into the living room like swirling dancing girls. From the kitchen Kessa could hear the faint sounds of the radio. She thought of going straight to her room but knew her mother had heard the sound of the front door closing.

As Kessa entered the kitchen, her mother looked up from the letter she was reading. "How was class?" It was clear from the speed with which Grace Dietrich returned to the letter that she had anticipated the daughter's answer.

"Fine," Kessa said.

"Anything unusual?"

"Francesca Louise Dietrich died! Kessa lives!" She wanted to scream the words that would tear her mother from the letter—it would be from her sister or brother, Kessa knew—but she merely murmured, "Nothing special."

Kessa watched her mother's face as she read. From the way her complexion, normally pale against the blond hair, flushed as her eyes traveled down the page, Kessa guessed the letter was from Susanna. Gregg's letters from Harvard always made her mother beam with pride. He had gotten another A, won another award, been elected to another office. In fact, the only thing about Gregg's letters that didn't please her mother was their frequency, or rather, infrequency. Grace never said a word to anyone, but Kessa knew her mother waited for Gregg's calls and letters with the eagerness of a young girl waiting for an invitation to a prom. And they came with about as much regularity.

"What does Susanna have to say?" Kessa asked.

"She's thinking of leaving this commune and moving to another near Big Sur. She says she's beginning to get 'bad vibes' at this one." Grace was wondering whether the "bad vibes" were drug-induced.

When Susanna had quit college and gone to live in a California commune, Grace Dietrich had told herself she was through worrying about her older daughter. She had always been a problem, always the child contemptuous of her advantages. But, of course, Grace couldn't stop worrying about her any more than she could stop breathing. Even in her absence, Susanna dominated her attention. And though she wouldn't admit it to herself, she had a certain grudging respect for Susanna's spunk. Francesca, on the other hand, was never a problem. She looked at the slight, fair girl before her.

"You must be hungry, Francesca. There's some apple pie from last night in the fridge."

Kessa went cold at the words. "I had something to eat after class." The lie was a suit of armor that might crack any minute, and she felt the need to get away from her mother immediately. "I think I'll get started on my homework. I've got an English test tomorrow."

There's no doubt about it, Grace thought as she watched the slim, straight back disappear down the hall. Francesca's too good to be true. I never even have to remind her to do her homework. She's so independent I don't even know she's there sometimes. Not like Susanna, and the endless battles over what seemed to be everything. She turned back to the letter.

Kessa closed the door to her room. She knew her mother would not bother her until dinner was ready. As she put her books on her desk, she noticed that the cleaning woman had rearranged her blotter and the pencils in the small Harvard mug Gregg had sent her two years ago. Kessa could feel the rage rising within her. She had told her mother again and again that she would take care of her own room. She didn't want that old cow shuffling around and getting her things out of order. Every time the cleaning woman rearranged her possessions, Kessa felt as if her whole life were out of order, as if she had no control over anything. She moved the blotter to the exact center of the desk and placed the small mug to the upper right-hand side of it. Then she walked to the mirror on the back of the closet door. She stood very close so that her nose was almost touching its reflection. Turning so that she would see her face in profile, she touched one cheek, then turned to view the other cheek and probed that with her fingers. Where were the bones, the ones those models on the magazine covers had? Despite her exhaustion she was glad she had walked the thirty blocks home. That must count for something.

Kessa took a step back from the mirror and pulled her leotard down to her waist. Her breasts were small enough so that she did not have to wear a bra, but they were still too large. *Useless fat*, Kessa thought. *They'll have to go.* She remembered the lamb chops she had seen defrosting on the kitchen counter, the peeled potatoes soaking in water. They were the enemy, but she had beaten the enemy once today and she would do it again. Fran-

15

cesca may have given in to Charlie's Soup Burg and meat and potatoes, but Kessa would not. She began to plan. She would eat no potatoes and only one chop. Kessa raised her arms above her head and took a deep breath. Her ribs made prominent ridges in the smooth skin. The sight was reassuring.

Kessa thought she might study for the English test—she was determined not to lose her A average—but after the long walk uptown the bed looked inviting. She took off her shoes and arranged herself precisely in the middle of the bed. *Just a little nap before dinner,* she thought. At least it would stop her from thinking about food.

"Dinner." The word sliced into Kessa's sleep and brought her back to the nightmare ahead. She turned over on her back and slid her hand down to her stomach. Flat. But not flat enough. It had to be concave. She had to have a margin for error, the error of eating too much.

"Francesca, dinner's ready!" Her mother's voice came down the hall like a call to battle. Kessa found the panic rising within her. They were going to force her to eat. Her stomach would swell grotesquely, her ribs would recede into a mass of flesh, and there was nothing she could do about it. But that was silly. Kessa was in control. They couldn't make Kessa eat. She marched down the hall toward the dining room to her own beat. *Kessa, Kes-sa, Kes-sa.*

Her parents were already at the table. "You must have been awfully engrossed in that English," her mother said. "That was the third time I called you."

Kessa rubbed her eyes and said nothing.

"It looks as if Francesca was sleeping instead

of studying." There was no harshness in Hal Dietrich's loud voice—he knew he did not have to worry about his younger daughter's grades—but neither was there any kindness. Kessa heard the tone, saw the drink next to his plate, and knew her father had come home angry. She wondered what it was this time.

"I tell you, Grace," he said as he began to heap food onto Kessa's plate, "I have half a mind not to send her any money."

Kessa watched the scalloped potatoes mount with a rising sense of alarm. She had to have a battle plan. *Kes-sa, Kes-sa.* It beat in her head. *One, two, three, four.* The magic number. She'd chant her name twice between each bite. She began to beat against the side of her chair with her fingers. *Kes-sa, Kes-sa.*

"Stop fidgeting, Francesca," her father snapped. "I work hard, Grace, and she doesn't do *anything*. Back to the land, she says. She's not back on the land. She's living on my money." He wanted his wife to know he couldn't be fooled.

"You're not going to change her by not sending money, Hal."

"She always cashes the checks."

Kessa heard her parents's voices as if from a distance. She saw their mouths going, her father's working angrily around the words, around the food he shoveled into it, her mother's pouting slightly, nibbling daintily, and felt as if she were watching them through a glass wall. She felt no connection with them, the words they were spewing out, or the food they were taking in. She was disconnected, miles away, safe.

"Francesca!" Her father's voice shattered the

protective wall. "Are you going to eat or are you just going to sit there in a daze all through dinner?"

"I am eating." She began to push the food around her plate.

"You may be moving the food around," her father said, "but you are definitely not eating."

"I don't like lamb chops." Kessa felt her mother's sudden attention.

"What do you mean, you don't like lamb chops? You used to love lamb chops."

"Well, I don't care whether you like lamb chops or not. Your mother made lamb chops for dinner and you'll eat lamb chops for dinner."

Kessa cut a minuscule piece of meat and raised it to her mouth. As she chewed, her fingers tapped out the magic formula on the side of her chair. *Kes-sa, Kes-sa.*

Kessa felt her father's eyes on her. "One mouthful does not a dinner make. I said you're going to eat your lamb chops, and you're going to eat them."

"Perhaps she doesn't feel well, Hal."

Now both parents had focused their attention on her, and Kessa began to eat rapidly. The chant now accompanied the tiny portions that she raised to her mouth in quick staccato movements. Suddenly she wiped her mouth with her napkin and stood.

" 'Scuse me," she mumbled, and walked quickly down the hall to the bathroom.

Kessa closed the door behind her and turned on both water faucets. Bending over the toilet, she stuck out her tongue and reached as far back in her throat as she could with her index finger. The first two times she merely gagged. On the third attempt she felt her stomach heave. Despite the pain, there was a surge of relief as the undigested dinner spewed out of her. *Empty again*, she thought, and flushed the toilet with a feeling of satisfaction.

"What's for dessert?" she asked as she returned to the table. The question, typical of the old fat Francesca, would hide the new Kessa from them.

"First you won't eat at all, then you gobble it down as if we're going to grab it away from you, and you can't wait for the next course." But there was no real anger in her father's voice. Francesca had followed his dictates and eaten her dinner. She was once again the obedient Francesca he knew. Kessa waited for him to bring up Susanna again.

"The trouble with that kid is that she has no idea what an honest day's work is. We gave her everything, and she couldn't throw it away fast enough."

"Gregg didn't have to work for any of his advantages, and he appreciates them," Grace said.

"Gregg's different. Kid's got common sense besides being smart."

Kessa heard the old familiar praises dully.

"Always had a summer job at Harvard," Harold continued. "Even before he could get one in his own field, he found a way to make money."

Ah, yes, Kessa thought, tapping the spoon against her dessert dish rhythmically. *That's our Gregg. Not only the smartest one in the family, but a money-maker just like Daddy.*

"Would you please stop fidgeting, Francesca!" Hal snapped.

Kessa's spoon halted in midair, and for a moment the old panic returned.

"But Susanna," Harold continued, "when has Susanna ever made a cent? . . ."

Silently, surreptitiously, Kessa returned to her

19

counting, and her father seemed to grow smaller and smaller until she couldn't hear his words at all

The following night victory came so easily Kessa was almost disappointed. She had prepared herself for another battle of the dinner table, but contest was called on account of her father's absence.

"Your father won't be home until late, Francesca." Kessa could hear the rage her mother was trying to control.

Grace Dietrich never got angry. That was her husband's prerogative. Over the years, in a thousand subtle ways, Grace had taught Kessa exactly what she thought of showing anger. The lessons ranged from "A lady doesn't raise her voice, Francesca" to "You get more bees with honey than vinegar, Francesca." Kessa wasn't the only one who had received such instructions, but it seemed only she had taken them to heart. Susanna had screamed and Gregg had ignored them. Only she seemed to struggle and end up confused. Suddenly a picture of Madame came to mind. It must have been more than a month ago now, sometime in February. Not sometime, Valentine's Day. Two girls in the class had been behaving badly, whispering, giggling, not working seriously at all. Kessa remembered the fire in Madame's eyes, and she could still see the veins in her lower arm as she gripped the pointer she had stopped in mid-count. Madame stood there sending out messages of rage as surely as a homing beacon sends out directions. She stood there staring until the silence in the room became almost palpable. When she finally spoke, her voice was coldly deprecating. "I have room in my class and time in my life only for serious dancers. Miss Miller, Miss Denman, I would like you both to leave my class."

The scene had terrified Kessa, and for the next several classes she had worked twice as hard to please. Then she had gradually forgotten it, but it came back to her now as she stood watching her mother struggling to stifle her anger. For one crazy moment she put Madame in her mother's place. "Mr. Dietrich, I do not accept your excuse for dinner. Will you please leave my kitchen."

"And I was going to make veal and fettucini."

Her mother's words burst the fantasy of her father's being called to task and sent a bolt of fear through Kessa. Fettucini. Butter and cream and pasta and a million calories conspiring to suffocate Kessa. Even the word was revolting.

"Of course, I can still make it for you now. I'm going to wait and eat later with your father."

The old dutiful Francesca merged with the new Kessa. "Don't bother, Mom. I'm not hungry now. I'll get started on my homework and make myself a sandwich later."

After her parents had eaten dinner and were in the living room in front of the television, her mother with her needlepoint, her father with his paper, Kessa went into the kitchen. She opened and closed the refrigerator several times, took a plate, a glass, and silverware noisily from the cupboards, filled the glass with water, and sat down at the table. She lifted the glass to her mouth, took a sip, and replaced the glass on the table. She repeated the procedure six times until she had drunk the entire glass. Suddenly Kessa felt happy, overwhelmingly, powerfully happy. *Water. Drink water. No calories, no preservatives, no carcinogens. No noth-*

21

ing. Drink water, water, and more water. She'd never get hungry, and she'd never get fat. Water. The magic formula. Kessa's salvation.

She sang as she carried the plate, knife, fork, and glass to the sink and put them in the dishwasher. She rejoiced at the squeaking noise the machine made as it closed. The sound would carry to the living room.

Kessa moved down the hallway to her room with small ballet steps in time to her name. She closed the door and carried the movement into three turns, perfectly executed turns, she thought. Then, flinging herself face up on the bed, she ran her hand over her stomach. Flat. She inhaled and looked down. There was at least an inch between her stomach and the waistband of her jeans. She reached beneath the jeans. The elastic waistband of her underpants lay flat against her stomach. Kessa felt a lurching panic. That shouldn't be. There should be a space between her stomach and underpants just as there was between her stomach and jeans. She would be more careful tomorrow. She had eaten nothing for lunch yesterday, but this afternoon as the girls had wandered out to the little grocery store to buy sandwiches and ice cream and Doodles and cokes, one of them had noticed that Kessa was not eating for the second day in a row. "Hey Francesca," she called over the noise of the crowd, "what's wrong with you anyway?"

The words sounded sharp and insistent in Kessa's ears. She wasn't like the rest of the girls. Something was "wrong with her."

"Nothing." Kessa laughed and bought a container of peach yogurt.

"You on a diet?" another girl asked.

"Kind of."

"But you don't have to diet. You're so thin."
The girl's voice was heavy with envy, and suddenly
Kessa felt much better. She ate the yogurt slowly,
repeating the words in her head. *So thin. So thin. So
thin.*

When the bell rang, summoning them back
into the building, the container was still half full.
Kessa tossed it into the trash basket with a feeling of
irrepressible joy. But the joy was gone now as she
felt the elastic tight against her stomach. There
would be no yogurt tomorrow. Tomorrow she'd think
up some excuse not to go with the girls to the
store at lunchtime.

Later that night, as Grace Dietrich made her
last tour of the apartment to turn out the lights,
she noticed that there were no dishes in the sink.
How many teenage girls would bother to put dishes
in the dishwasher? When Gregg and Susanna lived
at home, the kitchen had looked like the rummage
table of Bloomingdale's dishware department, with
pots and pans and glasses and plates tumbling
over each other in a cascade of half-eaten snacks.
Even then Grace remembered, Francesca had been
neat. What a pleasure to have a child who showed
some consideration for the rest of the family. What
a pleasure to have a child who allowed you to
worry about other things.

Kessa sat in the last row of the study hall,
slumped low with her head held forward, as if the
low profile would make her invisible. She was
smarting from Mlle. Boulanger's reprimand. Kessa
still didn't know what the question had been, but
when Mlle. Boulanger had called Kessa's name three
times and still received no answer, she had launched
into a sarcastic tirade in rapid-fire French. It was

23

only when every head in the class had turned to her that Kessa realized the teacher's diatribe was directed against her.

Kessa was stung by the words, only half of which she could comprehend through her own embarrassment and Mlle. Boulanger's perfect accent. French was one of Kessa's best subjects, though she did well in all of them. But more important, she admired Mlle. Boulanger, who was young and attractive and so wonderfully sophisticated with her French accent and her French clothes, and she wanted Mlle. Boulanger to admire her. But now Mlle. Boulanger thought she was a fool, a fool and a failure like the girls who never had their papers in on time and anglicized their *r*'s. Well, to hell with Mlle. Boulanger. *Merde* on Mlle. Boulanger. Francesca might have needed her approval, but Kessa did not.

Kessa tossed her French grammar into her book bag and took out a copy of *Glamour* she had bought during lunch while the other girls were stuffing themselves with pizza at the little stand across the street. She began to work her way through the magazine, tearing out the photographs of the thinnest models. When she reached the last page of the issue, she had a dozen pictures. Kessa's standards for thinness were strict. She arranged them in order of their weight, with the heaviest on top. Kessa decided that as she surpassed each model she would throw that picture away. *Soon I'll be thinner than all of you*, she swore to herself. *And then I'll be the winner. The thinner is the winner.* She felt a contraction in her stomach, almost as if it were echoing her words, but she would not be intimidated by hunger pangs, despite the fact that it was two o'clock and she had eaten nothing so far today but half a grapefruit. *The thinner is the winner*, she repeated, and smiled menacingly at the models, who grinned back at her in vacant pride at their own appearance.

2

Kessa lost four pounds that first week, and as if in reward Madame stopped her on the way out of class, "I'd like to speak to you about something, Francesca. I have only half an hour, and I definitely need a pick-me-up. Perhaps we could talk in the health-food store down the street."

Kessa's mind raced as she changed her clothes. Madame wanted to speak to her about something special. The idea was at once thrilling and terrifying.

Outside the studio on Fifty-second Street the landscape was familiar, but Kessa felt as if she had never really seen it before. Often, as she walked from class, Kessa pretended that it was her name up in lights over the theaters or her photograph staring down at the unimportant pedestrians from the huge glassed-in posters; but today, hurrying beside Madame through the intermittent patches of black shadow and brilliant sunshine that are New York on a bright March afernoon, she felt no need for such daydreams. What were the daydreams of stardom next to the reality of Madame? Oh, to be like Madame. To be Madame. She wanted to slide

27

inside the teacher's body. It seemed such a secure place to be.

Madame's manner was brisk. She had said little on their way to the restaurant, and only after she had ordered a sprout salad and large glass of grapefruit juice and Kessa had said she'd have juice too did Madame begin to speak.

"I can see you're taking my advice, Francesca."

Kessa held her breath for a moment. Did she dare? Yes, with Madame she dared anything. "My friends call me Kessa."

"An unusual nickname. Still, it sounds rather theatrical. Well, Kessa, I am glad to see that you're taking your body seriously. I shudder when I see the girls leaving class and heading for the nearest hamburger, coke, and French fry station. The thought of them pouring all those dead calories into themselves makes me want to cry. You'd think after a rigorous dance class they'd have more respect for their bodies."

Kessa nodded in eager agreement. She'd recently read an interview with a young ballerina, and she remembered it now. The girl had said that she was always so keyed up after a solo performance that despite the hunger and exhaustion, it took her at least two hours before she could eat anything and several hours before she could sleep.

"I'm usually too keyed up after class to eat much of anything at all."

Madame looked at the girl carefully. She had evaluated her physical abilities; now she was sizing up her spirit and determination. The comment about being too keyed up after class boded well. It was the response of a true professional. Madame could eat after the classes she taught, but when she had danced professionally she had never been able to eat immediately after a performance.

"Kessa, are you familiar with the special summer workshops, the studios run by the New York City Ballet, the American Ballet Theatre, and the Joffrey?"

Was Kessa familiar with them! As familiar as she was with the shape and scope of her own daydreams. "I think so," she said.

"Well, these studios do more than teach, Kessa. They sort and select. Young dancers come from all over the country every summer to study at these studios. Most of them return home better trained and with some memorable experiences. But memorable experiences are not what the dance is about. A handful, and only a handful, go on to the school's regular winter session. The very best of those can hope for a career in ballet.

"There are many requirements for recommendations to these summer studios. To begin with the body itself ..."

Kessa felt the grapefruit juice turn bitter in her mouth, but Madame dismissed the topic as rapidly as she had introduced it. "You've proved you're working on that. Then, of course, you have to be sufficiently advanced in technique and training. I've been watching your progress, Kessa, and while I wouldn't call it astounding, I do find it satisfactory. But perhaps the most important requirement—well, not the most important, but the one that puts it all together—is determination. Devotion to the dance, the sheer will to put it before everything else in your life. Tell me Kessa, do you think you have that kind of determination"

She thought of last week, of the birth of Kessa

and her growth and strengthening. As if it were a symbol, she pushed the glass of grapefruit juice away. "I think I do. I've been practicing more than ever, and I've been dieting—thinning and firming."

"Well, I think you do too, Kessa. And I'd like you to speak to your parents about it. If they agree, I'm going to recommend you for an audition."

The idea of an audition held no reality for Kessa at the moment. The only thing that mattered was that Madame had noticed her, Madame had selected her. She was Madame's choice, Madame's protégée, Madame's child. Kessa thought of her parents. She wouldn't bother to ask them. They knew nothing of Kessa, had no right to share in Kessa's triumph, had no right to come between Kessa and Madame. Finally someone cared about her and didn't worry about her brother and sister. The next dance class, she'd simply tell Madame she had spoken to her parents and that they were pleased.

3

Though Kessa had lost four pounds that first week, it took Grace two more to notice the change in her daughter's body. Perhaps that was because she was seeing less of her daughter these days. Francesca returned home from school or dance class and went immediately to her room. On most afternoons Grace heard the sound of ballet music on Francesca's stereo and the dull thuds of her daughter's practicing. On other afternoons she heard nothing. She supposed the girl was studying, but occasionally Francesca appeared at the dinner table red-eyed and listless, and Grace began to think she had been sleeping.

Francesca's behavior at the dinner table had changed too. She was withdrawn and answered her parents' questions with dull monosyllables. Often they had to repeat their questions. At those times Francesca would lift her eyes from the plate before her and look at her parents as if she had come from a great distance.

And there was no doubt in Grace's mind that Francesca wasn't eating properly. Each night she carried three dinner plates into the kitchen, but it looked as if only two people had eaten. Francesca's food would be cut up and arranged carefully, almost in a geometric pattern, but it would be *there*.

Grace watched Francesca come striding through the wide arch into the dining room. She was pleased that the girl had washed her face and combed her hair. Grace firmly believed that dining was just as much a matter of etiquette as of nutrition, and she had instilled that conviction in all her children. Hal had been indifferent to her concern, but this was one instance in which she had been firm enough to have her way. As Francesca sat down, Grace noticed that she still looked tired and somehow out of sorts. Her face was pale and thin, and her jeans bulked generously around her waist and behind. Grace remembered they had been skintight only last month.

"Have you been losing weight, Francesca?"

"Not really."

"Well, you certainly look as if you have."

"Maybe just a pound or two. After all, summer's coming, and I don't want to look gross on the beach."

"You've never looked gross in your life, Francesca, and you know it. And moreover, I don't want you dieting," Grace said as she heaped wild rice on her husband's and her daughter's plates, omitting her own.

Kessa did not miss her mother's action. "Why not? You're always dieting and you're thin."

"I'm not always dieting, Francesca. I merely watch my weight. After a certain age a woman has to, but you're a long way from that. If you don't eat properly at your age, you're sure to endanger your health."

Grace had always watched over her children's diet, mashing and pureeing their baby food and even eschewing commerical products full of chemicals. After all, her own mother had done so for her, despite a high-powered job in advertising and servants available for any task. Grace, who had no career, felt a special obligation to care for her children in this painstaking way. If you weren't a good wife and mother in her position, Grace reasoned, you weren't much of anything.

"I'm not endangering my health," Kessa sulked. "I never eat potato chips or soda or any of that garbage. I'm just cutting down a little, just to make sure my bikini fits."

Hal Dietrich had been listening to the conversation halfheartedly. He had carried his tired, somewhat overweight body uptown from his West Side office, but his mind had remained in the dusty room littered with invoices and brochures. He had worked hard for that office. Starting with nothing, not even a college education, he'd become one of the most successful jobbers of heavy industrial machinery in the East. He was proud of his accomplishment, so proud that it was sometimes hard to leave it behind at five-thirty and face the rest of the world. Today it had been frustrating, and now the dinner table conversation grated on his raw nerves.

"If your mother tells you not to cut down, Francesca, then you're not to cut down. Eat your dinner." The order seemed to settle the matter for Hal.

Kessa began to cut her meat into tiny pieces. As a whole it was unmanageable, frightening; but divided and arranged, the meat could be controlled. She cut four pieces. She'd count to four between each bite.

"I didn't say play with your food, Francesca. I said eat it."

Even Hal heard the curtness of his tone and quickly took a sip of the scotch he had carried in to dinner. Grace watched her husband and her daughter and wished she had never brought the matter up. She should have spoken to Francesca alone. It was always better when she spoke to her daughters alone. Hal was a conscientious father, working himself up from nothing to give his children every advantage Grace had ever had and more. And he loved them. Grace knew that from the way he worried about them and became impatient when anything went wrong. But sometimes, she couldn't help thinking, he didn't understand them very well. She resolved to talk to Francesca alone later this evening.

And Kessa decided she'd have to be more careful in the future. She felt so removed from her parents that she'd almost begun to think they couldn't see her. But of course they could, even if half the time they acted as if they weren't looking. She'd have to put up a better front at dinner, make it seem as if she were eating more than she was.

After Grace had scraped the plates—Francesca's still full despite Hal's careful overseeing of her dinner ("Eat that meat, Francesca; you haven't touched your string beans, Francesca; you're not going to get fat on salad, Francesca")—stacked the dishwasher, and cleaned up the kitchen, she made her way down the long hall hung with framed snapshots of the family. Here were twenty years of Dietrich history: the impossibly young-looking couple, the small children together and apart, then everyone growing older. She stopped for a moment in front of one photograph: she and Hal stood together, Susanna on one side, Gregg on the other, all smiling broadly. In the center in front of them

34

sat Francesca, small and serious-looking in her stroller. Grace touched the glass lightly and turned toward Francesca's room. Knocking on the door, she walked in without waiting for an answer. The girl had been lying on her bed, and she sat up with a start.

"You might at least wait for an answer. Don't I have any privacy in this house?"

Grace was startled by the anger in her daughter's tone, but more than that she was shocked by her appearance. In her jeans she had looked thin. Now, in her cotton underpants and the small bra she had never really needed, she looked dangerously underweight. Grace spoke more abruptly than she meant to.

"Look at what you've done to yourself, Francesca! You've got to stop this dieting foolishness and start eating properly."

"I told you, I have been eating properly." Kessa's mouth felt sour with the lie and taste of bile. After her father had forced her to betray herself, after she had stuffed herself with the unwanted food that made her want to cry, she had gone to the bathroom and stuck her finger down her throat. Kessa had brushed her teeth afterward, but her mouth still tasted funny.

"Well, if you're eating properly and you're still losing weight, there must be something wrong with you. I'll make an appointment with Dr. Gordon for a checkup.

"But I just went to Dr. Gordon two months ago."

Kessa remembered the appointment vividly. Dr. Gordon had put Francesca—Kessa had not yet been born—on the scale. She had watched the doctor slide the heavy metal weights against the

35

measured bar. "Ninety-eight pounds," Dr. Gordon had said rather as if she was announcing the results of a contest. "You could stand to gain a few pounds but someday you'll probably be worrying about losing them, so why bother. You're suffering from a severe case of good health, Francesca. See you next year." The news that she would probably have to worry about taking weight off someday had sent a wave of fear almost like nausea through her. For days after that she wondered just how soon she would have to begin worrying.

"If you're eating properly and losing weight, I think you ought to go to Dr. Gordon again," Grace repeated. "I'll call for an appointment tomorrow morning."

As she walked back down the hall to the living room and sat down across from Hal, or rather from Hal's newspaper, Grace remembered how Francesca had looked when she opened the door. Her hand had been lying on her stomach, and when she sat up there was an unmistakably guilty look on her face. Had the child been masturbating? If so, Grace's intrusion had been especially offensive. She resolved to say something to Francesca as casually as possible, to indicate that there was nothing wrong with experimenting with her own body.

"Did you settle the great dieting issue?" Hal's voice intruded on her thoughts. "Has she agreed to stop being foolish?"

"I'm going to take her to Dr. Gordon. If you and I tell her she's getting too thin"—Grace remembered the skinny figure on the bed and was glad Hal did not know just how thin Francesca had grown— "she doesn't pay any attention. It's the age, Hal. Everything we say is suspect. But if Dr. Gordon tells her she's getting too thin and backs it up with hard cold figures on a medical scale, maybe it will mean something."

Hal didn't have much patience with doctors—unless you were damn sick, that is—but in this case he thought his wife might be right. Someone had to talk some sense into the child. Damn kids these days, dieting themselves skinnier and skinnier so they could walk around the streets half-naked in obscenely tight T-shirts and see-through halters. Not that he had to worry about that sort of thing with Francesca. She was too young, and anyway she wasn't that kind of kid, not like her sister. He remembered an argument he'd had with Susanna. She'd been wearing a T-shirt which had written across it "Why don't we do it in the road." In one of his rare triumphs over his daughter, the shirt had gone back to the store.

"Maybe," he said, turning on the ten o'clock news and lowering his large, sturdy frame into his favorite chair, "the doctor can give her an appetite tonic or something like that. You know, something to make her eat." And the worries about Francesca's weight soon paled before the chronicle of violence, suffering, and economic dislocation that had suddenly invaded the Dietrich living room.

In the taxi on the way to Dr. Gordon's office, neither Kessa nor her mother said much. Grace was relying on the physician to do her persuading for her, and Kessa was too apprehensive to speak. Dr. Gordon would see her in her underwear. Worse yet, Dr. Gordon would read the numbers on the scale, and scales, especially scales in doctors' offices, didn't lie.

"Well, this is a surprise." Dr. Gordon addressed herself to Francesca rather than to Mrs. Dietrich. One of the reasons her pediatric practice included so many adolescents was her ability to treat them directly rather than through their parents. "I saw you a couple of months ago, Francesca. What's the problem?"

"There is none," Francesca said quickly.

"It's her weight," Grace interrupted. "Francesca's been losing too much weight. You can see that just by looking at her, but she insists she isn't dieting. If she's not dieting and she's still losing weight, I am sure there must be something wrong."

"Are you dieting, Francesca?"

"Just a little."

"I'm sure you've lost more than a little weight, Francesca," her mother said.

"There's one way to find out. The first thing to do is weigh you." Dr. Gordon did not miss the alarm on the girl's face any more than she had missed the exchange between mother and daughter. It was charged with suppressed anger of a sort the doctor had never seen between them before.

"Well, if I'm going to have any kind of an examination, I think it ought to be private." Kessa looked pointedly at her mother.

"Would you mind leaving the room for a moment, Mrs. Dietrich? We'll have a word after I examine Francesca. And Francesca, will you go into the dressing room, please, and get undressed. There's a gown in there."

Dr. Gordon watched the small, slight figure across the office. Her mother was right. She had lost a good deal of weight.

"Just how strenuously have you been dieting, Francesca?" Dr. Gordon asked her when she emerged in the short white gown. The tone was kind and held none of Grace's reproach.

"Not much. Honestly. Just enough not to look

gross in a bikini." Evelyn Gordon noticed Francesca's eyes did not meet hers as she answered.

Kessa stood on the scale praying it would lie for her and knowing it would not. Dr. Gordon moved the weights on the scale until the bar balanced. The result confirmed her fears. First Mrs. Dietrich's uncharacteristic carping manner, then Francesca's evasiveness, and now the concrete evidence.

"Eighty-eight pounds, eight ounces. That isn't very much, Francesca."

"I'm not very tall."

Dr. Gordon began to take her blood pressure. "When was your last period?"

"Six weeks ago. I guess I'm a little late." Kessa saw the look on Dr. Gordon's face. "Oh, I'm not pregnant. I couldn't be."

Dr. Gordon smiled. "That wasn't what I was thinking, Francesca, but it's nice to know we can rule out the possibility." She continued to examine Kessa while she talked. "A late period can tell you more about your body than the fact that it might be pregnant. I'm going to send you to a lab for some tests, but in this case I have a feeling your period is sending you a very simple message. I think it's telling you that you can't afford to weigh this little. As I said, we'll run some more tests just to make sure, and I want to see you again in two weeks. In the meantime, I don't want you to lose any more weight." The last statement was neither a threat nor a plea but a simple medical order.

Kessa left the office confused and angry. She had forgotten about her period and hadn't dreamed for a moment that it would be the thing to give her away. Her stupid period had tripped her up.

She hated her period, had hated it since it had appeared a little less than two years ago. Kessa could remember the day vividly. She had come home from dance to find the telltale stain. It had gone through her pants and her leotard. She was lucky it hadn't gone right through her skirt, a dark statement to the world of the terrible thing that had happened to her.

Kessa hadn't told her mother that day, or for months afterward. Somehow it seemed very important that her mother not know. If she did, if she knew that Kessa had stopped being a dependent little girl who needed her desperately, her mother would stop loving her. Kessa was sure of that. It had been the same when her breasts had begun to develop. Kessa had not let her mother see her without clothes for almost a year after that. If she had seen her body, had seen her become a woman, her mother would not have wanted to take care of her anymore. So she'd been delighted when her breasts had begun to shrink and her period had ceased to appear. Until today. Today her period, or rather its absence, had tripped her up, given her away. If only she had lied, if she had said her last period was just a week or two ago, Dr. Gordon wouldn't have had a weapon. *It's telling you that you can't afford to weigh this little.* Kessa was indignant. Her body sent its own messages, and they had nothing to do with Dr. Gordon or her period. She had always liked Dr. Gordon, but she resolved to be more careful with her in the future.

Entering the office, Grace looked no more confident than her daughter had leaving it.

"I think we can rule out any serious physical problems, Mrs. Dietrich, though I'm going to send Francesca to a lab for a few tests. I think the weight loss is deliberate. She seems to be dieting excessively, but that could present problems of its own." It was too soon for Evelyn Gordon to speak the words that she suspected diagnosed Francesca's problem. "I told her I wanted to see her again in two weeks and didn't want her to lose any more weight in the interim. Try to enforce that, and keep an eye on how much she eats, sleeps, and exercises."

"I've been trying to, but she's become so distant lately. It's hard to keep track of her at all."

"Distant?"

"She barely speaks to her father or me. When she's in the house—and that's almost never, now that she takes five dance classes a week—she stays locked in her room exercising or studying. Or at least she says she's studying."

"Well, if she's dancing five times a week and exercising, you might suggest that she eat more to offset the calorie loss."

"I've tried, but it always ends in an argument, and I don't want to sound as if I'm bullying her."

"Mrs. Dietrich, Francesca is fifteen years old. You're her mother. If she's doing something foolish, dangerously foolish, and you tell her to stop, you're not bullying her. You're fulfilling your responsibility as a parent."

"You make it sound so rational."

"That's because I'm not her mother."

And I never wanted to be, Grace thought, but did not say so to Dr. Gordon. She hadn't planned to have Francesca. Two children, a boy and a girl, were enough. She had the perfect family—then she'd gotten pregnant with Francesca. And now she was being punished for never having wanted her. But not never, Grace reassured herself. Once Francesca was born, she'd wanted her, cared for her, loved her as she had her other children. It had been so easy

41

to love Francesca. She had always been such a good child. But try as she might to rationalize her feelings, the guilt was still there. Somehow, in some minor—but lethal—unconscious way, she must have shown she hadn't wanted her. Whatever was wrong with Francesca must be her fault.

"It isn't your fault."

"What?"

"I was watching your face, Mrs. Dietrich. When a child has problems, parents tend to blame themselves. What did I do? What didn't I do? There are no answers there, and you're only going to wear yourself out trying to find them. Use the energy to try to help Francesca keep from losing any more weight. And I'll see you in two weeks. By then we'll have the results of the tests and know if the weight loss has stopped."

"And if it hasn't?"

"There's no point in anticipating the worst, Mrs. Dietrich. If Francesca is still losing weight then, we'll have more information to plan a course of action."

Both mother and daughter were silent in the taxi on the way home. For the first time in weeks Kessa was not thinking of food. She was thinking of her period. Could she will it to appear? Was there any way she could bring it on without gaining weight? It seemed terribly important that her period arrive before she saw Dr. Gordon again. It would prove that Dr. Gordon and the scale were both wrong. She was not losing too much weight. Six models she had clipped from a magazine that day in study period remained in her drawer. Six models had to be vanquished before Kessa could be proclaimed the winner.

"What would you like for dinner, Francesca?"

Grace was thinking that one way to keep her daughter from losing more weight was to tailor all meals to her taste.

Kessa's mind raced. Something simple, small, comfortable. "An egg."

"An egg? Dr. Gordon said you're not to lose any more weight. And she suggested you eat more to compensate for all those calories you burn up dancing and exercising."

"Well, I didn't go to dance class today, I went to Dr. Gordon. So I don't have to compensate for anything."

"All the same, an egg doesn't sound like much of a dinner." Grace's voice was defensive, a direct response to her daughter's accusation: *you* made me go to the doctor, *you* made me miss dance class, so don't go nagging me now about eating.

"I'll have some toast with it." One piece of toast, Kessa was thinking, sixty calories divided in quarters. She'd eat one quarter of the toast. Fifteen calories.

"Well, if that's what you want," Grace said uncertainly. "I'll make you bacon and eggs and toast."

Bacon. Fattening, greasy bacon, fifty calories a slice. A new wrinkle. Kessa began to grapple with the problem of dividing up the bacon—and still making it look as if she had eaten.

They got out of the taxi a block from the apartment. "I think we're out of butter," Grace said. "It'll just take a minute." The store was next to a pizza stand, and Kessa felt her stomach lurch at the aroma.

You are not hungry, she told herself, and began to chant *Kes-sa, Kes-sa*, in her mind. The spasm passed, and she felt strong and victorious. She had

43

kept control of her appetite and her body, and Kessa's world was in order.

In the elevator Mrs. Stone pushed the hold button until Grace and Francesca were on. "How's the prima ballerina today?" Mrs. Stone often saw Kessa coming from class carrying her book and the omnipresent dance shoes.

"Fine," Kessa mumbled, and kept her eyes on the ground. If she raised them, they would be exactly on a level with Mrs. Stone's obvious and unavoidable cleavage. A heavily boned bra pushed her breasts up and out, and the low-cut jersey top revealed two mountains of tired white flesh pressed firmly together to form a narrow valley. Kessa could not bear to look at her.

"You know, Francesca," Mrs. Stone said as the door opened on her floor, "you'd be an attractive girl if only you weren't so skinny."

"Fat bitch," Kessa murmured as the door scraped closed behind Mrs. Stone.

"She meant well, Francesca. And you see, everyone thinks you're too thin."

"Since when is Mrs. Stone an authority on appearance. I've heard you say a thousand times that she looks like an old hooker."

"I never said anything of the sort. What I said was that she wears too much makeup and her clothes are indiscreet."

"Which means she looks like an old hooker. Well, if that's the way a woman is supposed to look, I'd rather be too skinny." Kessa felt a flash of pleasure at the argument. Just let her mother try to push food into her now.

Harold was sitting in the living room when they arrived. There was an empty glass beside him.

Kessa wondered whether he'd had more than one drink, but Grace knew from the level of the bottle on the bar table that he'd had several. Hal always had a drink when he got home from the office, but when he'd had several and then continued to drink through dinner, it usually meant trouble—trouble at the office, and trouble later in the evening for someone in the family. Until a year ago, that someone had usually been Susanna, but tonight Kessa had the feeling she was in line for the honor.

"What did the doctor say, Francesca?"

Grace could feel herself begin to tremble. Taking responsibility was one thing, threatening and bullying something else; and the tone of Hal's voice was definitely bullying.

"Perhaps we could talk about it after dinner." And after you've got some food in your stomach to counteract the scotch, Grace was thinking.

"I didn't ask you, Grace. I asked Francesca. What did Dr. Gordon say?"

Kessa watched the superiority she had gained from the argument about Mrs. Stone melt like the ice in her father's glass. "She said if I'm going to diet I ought to do it carefully."

"Diet carefully. You're already skin and bones. Either you're lying, Francesca, or that lady doctor's crazy."

"Or you're drunk," Kessa threw back. "You always shout when you're drunk."

"I'm not drunk." In fact Hal was just short enough of being drunk for his daughter's words to sting. "All right, we'll discuss it after dinner. What's for dinner anyway?"

"Well, Francesca wants bacon and eggs."

"Bacon and eggs!" He glared at Francesca.

Why doesn't he just leave me alone! Kessa thought. *He never cared what I ate before. He never cared what I did before.*

"Don't worry, Hal," Grace intruded. "I'll make a steak for us."

"Since when does everyone in the family have something different for dinner?"

"Everyone isn't having something different for dinner. You and I are having steak, and I'm going to make some bacon and eggs for Francesca. It's no trouble, really." Grace's eyes pleaded with him. *Let it go, Harold, please let it go. As long as Francesca eats.*

"That was a good steak, Grace," Harold said when he'd finished his meal. The comment was the closest Hal ever came to apologizing.

Then he noticed Francesca's plate. He had kept his eyes from it during dinner because the very sight of it angered him. He did not believe in spoiling children, and giving in to a whim like Francesca's to have breakfast for dinner when there was a perfectly good steak was definitely spoiling her. He looked at the plate now and was infuriated, as much by the idea of the bacon and eggs as by the fact that they were still there. Francesca had divided the mound of scrambled eggs in four sections, cut the toast in quarters, broken the bacon in little pieces and arranged them in four piles, but she had eaten nothing.

"I thought you wanted bacon and eggs, Francesca. You haven't touched them."

Kessa heard the edge of anger in his voice, and the fear of the food on the plate before her mingled with the familiar dread of her father's outbursts. "I

46

guess I'm just not very hungry tonight. It must be the doctor's office."

"You asked for bacon and eggs and you got bacon and eggs. If your mother went to all the trouble of making you a special dinner . . ."

"It was no trouble, really, Hal," Grace interrupted.

"If your mother went to all the trouble of making it, you can do her the honor, your ladyship, of eating it." Kessa began to push the food around on her plate. "Eat your dinner, Francesca!"

She began to eat quickly now, in minuscule bites, but suddenly it seemed very important that none of the food on the fork touch her lips. The food on her lips would make her unclean. She removed each morsel from the fork with her teeth, then wiped her mouth with her napkin.

Grace watched her daughter in horror. It was as if she weren't eating at all but rather playing out some terrible pantomime. Grace was relieved when it was over, especially since Francesca had eaten most of her dinner for the first time in weeks. Kessa excused herself.

"Don't you want dessert?" Grace asked.

"I'm stuffed." It was not entirely a lie. Kessa had shrunk her stomach in the last weeks, and in addition to the feeling of being full there was another more terrifying one, as if a hundred appetites were raging out of control within her. She couldn't explain it, but she felt as if everything was in chaos and something awful was going to happen. She had eaten, and now something terrible would occur. Kessa had to get rid of the food immediately.

As she walked down the hall to the bathroom, her back was straight and her movements rigid.

She locked the door and turned on the water so her parents would not hear her. Then she rid herself of the unwanted food, washed her face, brushed her teeth, and went to her room.

The books piled neatly in the center of her desk caught her attention. She was two assignments behind in French, one in math. She'd never been behind in school in her life. It was an alarming feeling, but not nearly so alarming as the unwanted food. Had she really gotten rid of all of it? Were there remaining calories lurking inside her?

Kessa turned her back on the books. They really weren't important after all. She walked to the stereo and put on the Russian folk music record she'd bought when she'd gone to see the Bolshoi several months ago. She began to dance. As the pace of the music quickened, Kessa whirled and jumped and leapt until she was dizzy with movement and fatigue.

When Grace had finished cleaning up after dinner, she found Harold waiting for her in the living room. "Now, what's the real story, Grace? What did Dr. Gordon say?"

"Well, to begin with, she said there's nothing wrong with Francesca. Or rather nothing physically wrong. She wants Francesca to have some lab tests just to make sure, but she's pretty sure everything's okay."

"Nothing physically wrong. What are you trying to tell me—that there's something psychologically wrong? There's nothing wrong with Francesca's head. We know that. Susanna's the screwed-up one."

Grace forgot about Francesca and thought how Hal's belligerence made her stubborn sometimes. "Well, you never helped her, fighting the way you did."

"What was I supposed to do? She never wanted to discuss; she always just announced. She never asked me anything; she told me. And I'll tell you something. I'm the last one in this family she listens to."

He was right of course, Grace thought, but sometimes it seemed that Susanna and Hal's hostility hid a closeness more intense than anything she shared with her.

"Well, Susanna isn't the problem now, Francesca is. Dr. Gordon said she's dieting excessively and she's got to stop. She said she shouldn't lose any more weight and that we should keep an eye on how much she sleeps and exercises."

"That's all? That's Dr. Gordon's high-priced medical advice? She shouldn't lose any more weight and we should watch her sleep and exercise. Terrific!"

"Now, in the first place don't start on one of your doctor tirades again. Dr. Gordon isn't so high-priced, even if her office is on Park Avenue."

"I don't understand why they all have to specialize. What happened to the good old GP?"

"The same thing that happened to the black death and smallpox, I guess. God, Harold, there's more medical knowledge, so doctors specialize more. But that isn't the point. We start out talking about Francesca, and the next thing I know, we're arguing about Susanna or doctors or God knows what."

"All right then, what are we going to do about Francesca?"

"Dr. Gordon wants to see her again in two weeks."

"Why? If there's nothing wrong with her, why does she want to see her again in two weeks?"

"To check up on her. To make sure she hasn't lost any more weight."

"And what if she has? What does Dr. Gordon plan to do then?"

"Harold, why don't we wait till that happens —if it happens."

"I haven't gotten where I am in this world, Grace, by waiting for surprises. You have to plan a course of action. You have to be prepared."

"We're not talking about a business deal. We're talking about our daughter."

"That's exactly my point. She's our daughter, and I want to know what we're going to do if she goes on losing weight this way."

Grace looked at her husband. His voice had been harsh, yet there was nothing but concern in his eyes—concern he might not be able to reveal, but concern as real and strong as Grace's own.

"Dr. Gordon didn't say, Hal, and frankly I don't know. All we can do is wait. And in the meantime we're just going to have to cope with Francesca."

"Cope with Francesca. We've never had to cope with Francesca. We cope with Susanna, not Francesca."

"Well, now we're going to have to cope with Francesca, Harold, and that's all there is to it."

On her way from the bathroom to her room, Kessa overheard her parents' words. Susanna was the one they coped with, all right. They had always been so busy fighting with Susanna that half the time they hadn't even noticed Francesca.

She remembered an argument she'd overheard some time ago. It was late Saturday night, and her parents had been in their room with the early edition of the Sunday *Times*. Kessa had gone into Susanna's room to borrow a record. Of course

Susanna wasn't home. Pretty, voluptuous, rebellious Susanna wouldn't be home on a Saturday night. On the way back to her room, Kessa had heard her parents' voices. Once she realized what they were talking about, she had stood in the hall listening.

"Another report on the dangers of IUDs," her mother said. "I keep telling myself I'm going to give up reading these articles. All they do is frighten me."

"Why are you frightened?" Kessa could tell from her father's tone that he wasn't paying attention. "You don't have an IUD."

"I was thinking of Susanna."

"Susanna!" Now Kessa knew he was listening. He always listened about Susanna. "She's barely seventeen."

"These days seventeen isn't as young as it used to be. She asked if she could see a gynecologist."

"A gynecologist?"

"Yes. About birth control."

"Nothing doing." His tone sounded final. Kessa wished he would be as concerned about her.

"Look, Hal, be realistic. Susanna's going to sleep with someone soon, if she hasn't already. We can't stop her, so we might as well accept it and get her some protection."

Kessa listened to a firmness in her mother's voice. She always seemed strong when she defended Susanna.

"You're just condoning her behavior, and I won't allow it. I will not let my daughter sleep around, and that's that."

For Kessa, her sister's sexual habits—she knew Susanna had been sleeping with boys for at least six months—paled before her father's anger. That and the fact that her parents were arguing again,

51

arguing about Susanna. She had wanted to scream at them to stop. Stop the shouting and the crying and the cruelty. But of course she couldn't scream at them, because she wasn't supposed to be there.

Now, hearing her parents fighting again, Kessa remembered the years and years of bickering. She had always wondered how Susanna stood it, but Susanna not only endured it, she seemed to thrive on it. Well, Kessa wasn't going to thrive on it. She just wanted her parents to leave her alone. But even as she thought that, she experienced a small feeling of pleasure at the fact that for once her parents were fighting about her.

When Kessa got to her room, she locked the door behind her. She wasn't going to have her mother barging in again. After taking off her robe, she lay down on the bed. Kessa always felt her cleanest and thinnest right after she had showered, and tonight she felt especially good. True, she had been forced to eat dinner, but she had gotten rid of dinner. There was no food in her body. She was clean and pure and lean. Now for the test of how lean. Kessa ran her fingers over her stomach. Flat. But was it flat enough? Not quite. She still had some way to go. *Just to be safe,* she told herself. Still, it was nice the way her pelvic bones rose like sharp hills on either side of her stomach. *I love bones. Bones are beautiful.* She ran her hands up to her ribs and began to outline them carefully. *One, two . . .* the third was not sharp enough. There seemed to be a layer of tissue between her finger and the bone. There was no doubt about it. She still had a way to go. Kessa picked up her head and looked down at her breasts. Flatter, but still not flat enough. She lifted her left breast by the nipple and swayed it back

52

and forth. Floppy, too floppy. She'd have to exercise more.

Kessa thought of the English paper due tomorrow. She hadn't even read the play. Well, it was too late to do anything about it now. She'd just tell the teacher she hadn't finished the assignment. She'd always gotten away with that excuse in history. The teacher hadn't dreamed that Francesca, straight-A-always-has-the-answer Francesca, couldn't be bothered to do her homework.

Her mind felt tired when she thought of school, and her body ached with exhaustion, but the floppy breast and the flesh over the third rib had sent a current of fear through her. Kessa leapt up, turned on the phonograph, and began to dance—a frantic, desperate dance that would wash away the panic of that extra flesh.

4

That was the last party she'd go to, Kessa swore as she stomped up Central Park West. Her parents had made her promise that whenever she came home from a party alone she'd take a cab, but she was too angry to do that. She wanted to walk. Besides, the walk was good exercise. And from now on that's what she would do. She'd devote herself to the dance, as Madame did, and skip those kid parties. Kessa didn't know why she'd gone in the first place. She'd never been much good at parties, never been much good at friends, for that matter. It was such a struggle, wanting to be friends but then having to keep them at a distance.

For as long as she could remember, it had been that way. Kessa recalled the childhood games she used to invent. There would be a court and she would be the Queen. Her friends were the ladies-in-waiting, *her* ladies-in-waiting, and she would invent names for them. Maria Teresa. Elizabeth Anne. Katherine Lorraine. And her own name, her real name— the Queen's name—was the best of all. Francesca Louise. There was a time, long after she had stopped playing the game with her friends, when the memory of it could still make her feel warm and safe. She would walk through the halls of school or down Central Park West and pretend she was visiting royalty. Queen Francesca Louise had deigned to grace the city of New York with her presence. But the fantasy didn't work anymore, and now Francesca Louise was dead. Kessa lived in her place, and Kessa was a firm, strong girl, in command of her life. Kessa could do anything—except go to a party. But who wanted to go to that stupid old party anyway? She had said yes only because Julia had asked her. Julia was two years ahead of Kessa and very popular. All the girls looked up to her. Julia had never paid much attention to Kessa, but the other day after a modern dance class she had commented on Kessa's ability.

"Oh, it's nothing," Kessa demurred. "I mean, I ought to be able to do all that stuff. I take five ballet classes a week."

"Five classes a week. I guess you're going to be a professional dancer or something like that." Julia's tone was casual, but Kessa could see that she was impressed.

After that Julia began greeting Kessa in the halls, and once when they both had a free period she suggested they go down to the hamburger place for a snack. Kessa had ordered only black coffee, and when Julia's cheeseburger and coke came, she was glad they were sitting next to each other at a counter rather than across from each other at small tables. She didn't think she could stand to watch Julia consume the meal. Even out of the corner of her eye, the sight of Julia raising the burger to her mouth and taking great messy bites made Kessa dizzy. She told herself the dizziness was because she'd eaten nothing but a hard-boiled egg all day, but she knew the feeling came from something deeper and more frightening than that.

"I don't know how you do it," Julia said. "By this time in the afternoon I'm absolutely ravenous, and all you want is black coffee. But I guess that's why you're so thin." Julia was no slouch in the slender department herself, and Kessa took this last as a definite compliment. "But of course, if you're going to be a professional dancer you'd have to be." Julia continued. It was the final accolade, and so when Julia suggested that Kessa accompany her to this party tonight, she had been frightened but determined.

But when Julia had turned up at the agreed meeting place earlier this evening with two other girls—one from school, whom Kessa knew vaguely and did not like, and one whom she had never seen before—Kessa felt her confidence slipping away. She never should have agreed to come. She didn't belong with these girls. They were older and more sophisticated. As they walked down Park Avenue toward the party, they talked about the boy who was giving it.

"Reid's all right," Julia said.

"He's a turkey," the girl whom Kessa didn't like answered. "And that awful white body. Like mayonnaise. If I had known about that awful white body, I never would have slept with him."

Kessa knew from the way the girl said it that she was only showing off, but Kessa's superior knowledge did nothing to lessen the superiority of the other three girls. None of them seemed to notice Kessa's silence, so she walked along trying to look interested in the conversation and wondering how much worse things were going to get once they arrived at the party.

They got a lot worse. Julia abandoned her immediately, and the other two seemed never to have known her in the first place. The noise level was deafening, and Kessa only hoped the neighbors liked Kiss as much as the boy who lived here did. In the smoky darkness there were a lot of bodies leaning against walls, sprawling across the floor, and hanging on to each other, and a lot of joints and bottles being passed around. Kessa had never smoked pot, and she hated the taste of liquor. When kids teased her about this, she said it was because of the dance, and now, as she watched Julia across the room making a great scene of taking a drag from some boy's cigarette and the girl whom she didn't like trying hard to get drunk as quickly as possible, she told herself Madame would never sully her body with such things. But Kessa knew it was more than respect for her body that stopped her from getting stoned. It was fear for herself. There was something terrifying about losing control of herself.

Kessa found a corner and sat down with her back against a wall. It seemed like the safest place. She prayed that no one would bother her, but at the same time she hoped someone would. It seemed so terribly lonely to be sitting here among all these people who knew each other and who didn't know or care about her. She didn't belong here. She didn't belong anywhere. She had no one in the world. There was no one she could talk to, no one who understood the distance and the loneliness and the hard work of being perfect all the time No one understood and no one cared. Alone in the corner staring through the party which raged around her, Kessa could feel the tears welling up. She closed her eyes quickly to stop them before it was too late. She didn't know how long she had been sitting that way with her eyes closed, feigning some state of intoxicated bliss. It could have been three minutes or three hours.

"Hey, it's good stuff, isn't it? Pure gold."

Kessa opened her eyes to find a boy with long dark hair standing over her. It was clear that he believed it was the sheer joy of the grass rather than the fear of the party that had closed her eyes.

"My name's Mike. What's yours?" he said, sitting down next to her.

She hesitated for only a second. Julia knew her as Francesca, but Julia was nowhere in sight. "Kessa."

"That's a funny name." Her face must have shown something. "I mean, it's a nice name but kind of unusual. Like I'm Mike, and I guess that's about as usual as you can get." The thought seemed to depress Mike, and he took a deep drag from the joint he was holding. "Want some?"

"No, thanks. I'm high enough," she lied.

"Man, I can never get high enough. I mean, the higher I get, the better I feel. Don't you feel everything stronger when you're high. And the lights. I got a million lights going off in my head. Pop. Pop. Pop."

Kessa had heard it all before, and there never seemed to be anything to say in reply. "Mmm," she mumbled noncommittally.

Mike was obviously dissatisfied with the response, or lack of it. "Man, you really are on a bum trip, aren't you?"

Kessa shrugged her shoulders as if she didn't care what kind of a trip he thought she was on, and Mike drifted off. After he was gone she looked around wondering if anyone had observed the exchange. Two guys across the room seemed to be staring at her, and she was sure that at any minute they were going to come over and start telling her what a bum trip she was on and how she was a drag and didn't belong at the party, and then everyone would be staring at her and laughing at her and it would be all over school what a drag she was and how she never belonged anywhere. She had to get out before those two boys got to her. She had to. Quickly, pushing and stepping over people, crashing between them, she reached the door.

"Hey, Francesca." Julia was standing next to her. "You can't leave yet. We just got here."

Kessa began to mumble something about not feeling well, but Julia was already being dragged away by some guy who said she just had to hear this really terrific . . . Kessa stopped listening, just as Julia had stopped listening to her. She slammed the door behind her. *Bitch!* she thought. *Dumb little bitch!*.

That night Kessa dreamed of Madame. They were walking together to a movie. Madame bought the tickets and led Kessa inside to a huge lobby that looked like a dance studio. There were mirrors all around, and the barre, instead of being plain wood as it was at class, was red velvet, soft and plush and very regal looking. Kessa walked to the barre, but Madame shook her head and led her inside to the theater. There was a stage with a curtain in front. In place of the customary rows of seats stood the familiar furniture from her parents' apartment. The curtain parted, and Madame was no longer in the audience but up on the stage. Julia was there too, standing off to one side, and on the other side were Kessa's parents. They were all wearing leotards, and as Madame began to dance, a beautiful dance that beckoned Kessa to come up and join her on the stage, Julia and her parents began to follow with halting little steps. But they could not keep up with Madame, and as her movements became more difficult, more dazzling, the other dancers began to grow smaller and smaller. Suddenly the spotlight over Julia went out. And then, a moment later, as her parents tried to emulate Madame's magnificent arabesque, their lights went out too. Madame was dancing alone now, whirling, leaping and beckoning, always beckoning, and the spotlight that shone down on her grew brighter and brighter until Kessa thought it would blind her. Brighter and brighter and brighter, and then there was a terrible explosion and the room went dark and Kessa was alone in a black void.

Then the black void read a luminous 4:27, and Kessa realized she had opened her eyes and was staring at the digital clock radio on her night table. She was hot and covered with perspiration. Her hair stuck on her head, and the pajamas felt clammy against her body.

She lay for a moment staring up into the darkness. She couldn't recapture the dream, only the feeling of terror that had ended it. Then she remembered the party earlier that night. It must have been the pot, she decided. There was so much smoke floating around the room that she must have gotten high without realizing it. For the second time that night Kessa resolved there would be no more parties. She could not risk losing the control over herself that Kessa had fought so hard for.

5

When Kessa awakened the next morning, remnants of fear still clung to her just as sleep encrusts the eyes after a long night. She removed her pajamas and squared off with her image in the mirror for her regular morning drill. "Pull that stomach in!" Her voice was a whisper, but her tone was a bark. She turned sideways. Flat, but not flat enough. She raised her hands over her head and began to count the line of ribs. They stopped behind the wrinkled skin of her breast. "Disgusting," she hissed. "Absolutely disgusting. That isn't Kessa in the mirror. That must be Francesca." Of course. She thought she'd killed Francesca, but the little sneak had merely gone into hiding. Francesca had just been waiting for her chance to ambush Kessa, and last night at the party she'd gotten it. But this morning things were different. This morning Kessa was in control again. She lifted her left breast with her right hand and pinched it hard. The girl in the mirror began to cry. Francesca Louise began to cry. Two rivers of water streamed down either side of Francesca Louise's nose. "Coward," Kessa hissed at the crying girl. "Queen Francesca Louise, queen of the cowards, queen of nothing, queen of nobody. You're finished, ended, dead." Kessa was still pinching and the girl in the mirror was still crying. "Good-bye forever, Francesca Louise."

A half hour later Kessa walked to the bathroom and locked the door behind her. She brushed her teeth carefully, used a mouthwash, then examined her teeth in the mirror. *Good teeth,* she thought. *Clean teeth. Too clean for food. Food makes them dirty. No more food.*

Kessa looked at the toilet with disdain. She had purposely brushed her teeth first. She wanted to put off any contact with the toilet. It was unclean. Spreading her legs, she stood carefully above it. Kessa had taken to treating the toilet in her own bathroom as her mother had often advised her to treat those in public places, but this morning it suddenly seemed more important than ever that no part of her body touch the clammy, unclean enamel.

Kessa left the bathroom feeling pleased with herself. She had not touched the toilet. She had performed all the requisite rituals. For the moment at least, fear slept.

Later that morning when Grace was cleaning her daughter's bathroom, she found a stain on the tile floor right in front of the toilet. It was the third time that had happened this week. The first time she had thought that Harold had used Francesca's bathroom and been careless, but now she knew that was impossible. Harold had used their own bathroom that morning and then gone to his office. Grace thought of public toilet seats sprinkled with urine by women too impolite to lift the seat. It was the only explanation she could find for the stain on the floor. Francesca was standing over the toilet rather than sitting on it. One more item for her list: the lips drawn back so as not to touch the fork; the mouth wiped clean after every bite; the tapping of the fingers on her chair when Hal finally forced her to take some food. At first Grace had thought Francesca was merely fidgeting, but as they sat in strained silence meal after meal, the meaningless tapping became an intentional staccato beat.

Grace had made a mental list for Dr. Gordon, and now she could add urine stains to it. She had no idea what was the matter with her daughter, but she did know now with a stomach-tightening certainty that something was wrong.

As soon as Francesca entered her office, Dr. Gordon knew that the girl had not followed instructions. She was visibly thinner. The doctor hid her annoyance behind a hearty greeting and directed Francesca to the dressing room.

"We might as well start with the scale," she said when Kessa had emerged in the short white gown. "Hop on. How about your period, Francesca? Has it shown up?"

"Not yet." Kessa had been prepared to lie, but Dr. Gordon had caught her off balance. She had been so busy watching the weights, those telltale weights, that she had answered without thinking.

Dr. Gordon said nothing as she placed the larger weight at fifty and began to slide the smaller one down the bar. Thirty-four, thirty-three, thirty-two. *God*, Kessa thought, *won't it ever stop?* Finally Dr. Gordon's slender fingers brought it to a balanced rest at thirty-one.

"You weigh eighty-one, Francesca."

There was no mistaking the anger in the doctor's voice. *Well, let her get angry*, Kessa thought. *Madame approves. Madame says dancers ought to be thin.*

Evelyn Gordon saw the look of defiance that crossed the girl's face and wanted to slap her. The stupidity of it all. People starving to death all over the world, and this foolish child determined to ruin her health for . . . for what? For fashion? For attention? Evelyn Gordon reminded herself that she didn't know the answer, and that Francesca was not a foolish child but a sick one, as sick as if she had any of a hundred crippling physical diseases.

"You're still dieting, aren't you Francesca?"

"Only a little. I figure if I lose enough weight, then I won't have to worry at all, and I'll be able to eat anything I want."

Evelyn Gordon wanted to scream that Francesca had no idea what she really had to worry about. After all, Francesca had never heard of anorexia nervosa. Instead she said in a calm voice, "I told you not to lose any more weight, Francesca, yet you contine to diet. For some reason, you seem unable to resume normal eating habits."

"My eating habits are normal."

"Normal eating habits don't take a girl your age and size down to eighty-one pounds. I'm going to give you a prescription for some medication. It will give you more of an appetite. I think that's the first step."

Kessa was too terrified by the news of the medication to notice the rest of Dr. Gordon's statement. Could they force her to take the medication? She could picture her father standing over her now. And no matter how quickly she got to the bathroom, she'd never be able to throw all of it up. Traces of medicine would remain in her stomach, churning it up with an insatiable hunger, forcing her to eat against her will, forcing Kessa to give in to Francesca, forcing thin, self-controlled Kessa to become fat, fearful Francesca. Dr. Gordon's words, telling her to get dressed and send her mother in, cut through the haze of terror that engulfed her.

"I'm not happy about the picture, Mrs. Dietrich," Dr. Gordon said when Grace was sitting across the desk from her. "Francesca's lost more weight. About seven pounds in two weeks."

"We've tried to watch her," Grace said quickly. "We've tried to make her eat more and stop her from exercising too much."

"I'm sure you have. I wasn't accusing you."

Grace seemed not to have heard her. "But it's so hard. She's so distant. And so sullen now. I'm almost afraid to talk to her. And all those strange little habits."

"Strange little habits?"

"Well, not only how little she eats, but the way she eats." Grace went on to describe Francesca's full ritual. "And there's one other thing. I've never actually seen it, but I can guess what's happening." She told Gordon about the stains in the bathroom.

"Mrs. Dietrich, I think the time has come for Francesca to see a psychiatrist." There was a time when the word would have frightened Grace. Now it was merely anticlimactic. "I think there's a good possibility that she has anorexia nervosa. Do you know what that is?"

"I read an article about it several weeks ago. It sounded like what Francesca was doing, but I kept telling myself that was impossible. Francesca's not sick, at least not mentally sick. She's always been the sensible child, the good one in the family."

"It has nothing to do with being sensible or

67

good. You can't look at this as something Francesca has suddenly decided she's going to do—at least, not consciously decided. It's more complex than that. Much more."

"But I don't understand. What causes it? I tried to understand from the article, but I couldn't. I wish you'd explain."

"I wish I could. I've read dozens of articles, and everybody has an answer, but no one seems to have the right one. We do know it affects girls from good homes, upper and middle class. Then there's one theory about girls being afraid to grow up, so they try to keep their bodies childlike. But why are they afraid to grow up?" Dr. Gordon hesitated for a moment. "There's another school that says it has something to do with a mother-daughter power struggle, but for what it's worth, Mrs. Dietrich, I don't buy that one at all. To begin with, why should the girls take it out in starvation? And besides, there isn't a teenage girl—a healthy teenage girl, that is—who doesn't have some kind of a power struggle with her mother at some time. Then there's the brain lesion theory, but I've never heard of a lesion that affects only middle-class brains. I realize I'm not giving you much in the way of an answer, but I'm afraid this is one of those things medical science still doesn't have much of an answer for. All we really know is that it's a very serious disease that affects girls mostly between thirteen and twenty-eight—and that it's on the rise."

"Well, what about the physical part of it? I mean, what happens if Francesca goes on losing weight?"

Dr. Gordon didn't like the answers, but at least there were answers here. "They can lose up to twenty-five percent of their body weight. As a result they lose their periods too. Francesca is already a month overdue. If they continue to refuse to eat, their skin begins to dry out and their hair looks dull. There may even be some loss of hair—on the head, that is. They often grow more hair on the rest of the body."

"It sounds horrible." Dr. Gordon said nothing. "Just how horrible can it get? I mean, in the article I read the girl died." Grace's voice was almost a whisper. "Will Francesca die?"

Evelyn Gordon's tone was brisk. "Let's not jump to conclusions, Mrs. Dietrich." She debated giving her the figures. Would the woman concentrate on the fifteen percent who died or the eighty-five percent who lived? She decided there was no need to talk about death rates at this stage. "The important thing is to get Francesca to a psychiatrist as soon as possible. I'm giving her some medication, but to be perfectly honest, I don't have much faith in it. This is a psychological problem, and we're going to have to find a psychological solution to it—as quickly as possible." Dr. Gordon forced herself to look Grace Dietrich squarely in the eye. "If Francesca continues to lose weight, we're going to have to put her in the hospital."

The hospital. It had always been a terrible thing to Grace, except when she'd gone to have her children, but now there was something almost reassuring about it. A concrete answer to all the inexplicable questions. "Will the hospital make her better?"

"The hospital can keep her from starving herself. It can keep her alive. I think that's about all we can expect from physical medical procedures.

Now I can refer you to a psychiatrist, but before I do, I think we ought to talk this over with Francesca."

Dr. Gordon buzzed the receptionist and told her to send Francesca back in. As Grace waited for her daughter to return, the worry over Francesca's condition merged with guilt at her own past thoughts. Before this all started, Grace recalled, I thought about how in two years Francesca would be off to college and Hal and I'd be alone again. I'd have done my job, all the children would be on their own, and it would be the way it was when we were first married. Not as exciting, of course, but more peaceful. And private. Finally, after all these years, private. And now, she was convinced as she watched Francesca enter the office, pale and thin as a concentration camp inmate, I'm being punished for it.

Kessa listened sullenly to Dr. Gordon's words. When she said Kessa had a disease, something called anorexia nervosa, the girl knew she'd won. She had been afraid they'd find out, find out about the death of Francesca and her new self and new body and new code of behavior—but they hadn't. They thought she was sick, and now Kessa and her wonderful new body were safe agin.

"And if you continue to lose weight, Francesca, I'm afraid you'll have to go into the hospital." Dr. Gordon's words penetrated the safe coat of armor in which Kessa had dressed herself.

"What kind of a hospital?"

"A hospital that can keep you from losing more weight."

Kessa pictured herself tied and trussed in a straitjacket like that girl in the movie she'd seen several months ago. But instead of the actress it would be Kessa who would lose control of herself. She would not be able to move or fight back, and they would shovel food into her until she was huge and fat and repulsive.

"In the meantime, Francesca, your mother and I have discussed it, and we think the best thing would be for you to see a psychiatrist."

Kessa couldn't focus on Dr. Gordon's words any longer. It was a puzzle of broken phrases, and Kessa could not put them together to form a picture of what she was saying. Only two things were clear—that they had threatened her with a hospital and that she might be able to stay out of the hospital by going to the psychiatrist. The idea of a psychiatrist was frightening, but not nearly so frightening as the thought of going into a hospital.

By the time they reached the apartment, Grace's satisfaction at her daughter's willingness to see the psychiatrist had turned to anger. Francesca had seemed so reasonable in Dr. Gordon's office—sullen, but reasonable—that Grace was certain the girl was torturing them on purpose. And then, as she remembered the foolish eating habits and the bathroom behavior and the possibility that Francesca might starve herself to death, starve herself to death just to spite her mother, Grace's anger spiraled into rage.

"Did you hear what Dr. Gordon said?" she screamed when Francesca refused her offer of a glass of milk. "Do you want to go into a hospital? Are you so crazy that that's your idea of fun? Are you so crazy that you want to starve yourself to death?"

Kessa stared blankly past her mother. She had never seen her angry before, at least not this angry, but she didn't care. Her finger tapped out the magic formula against her thigh. *Kes-sa, Kes-sa, Kes-sa.* She

71

felt safe, safe and superior in the face of her mother's rage.

"Can't you speak, goddamn it! Can't you say anything?"

Kessa continued to stare blankly ahead, and her mother, blind with rage and tears, tears that she had been saving for two decades, pushed past her and ran down the hall to her own room. Kessa heard the door slam and then, for what seemed like a long time, her mother's sobs, only slightly muffled by the closed door and thick walls of the apartment. Somehow the crying gave her a feeling of satisfaction.

When Harold arrived home that night, he found his wife as he had not found her since the children were babies. Several times in the early years of marriage he had returned home to find Grace red-eyed from the frustrations of being locked up with two babies born within fifteen months of each other. But the children had grown, and Grace had learned to cope, and it had been a good many years since Harold had seen the aftereffects of an afternoon of tears. He was more resigned than angry. For the last two weeks he had tried not to think of Francesca or her problem, but he had always known it was there.

"I take it Dr. Gordon was not encouraging." Harold began pouring a drink as he talked. "Do you want one?"

Grace shook her head. She wanted to be as calm as possible when she broached the idea of a psychiatrist with Harold.

"Remember that article I told you I read? Well, Dr. Gordon thinks that's what Francesca has. An-

72

orexia nervosa." The term, once so difficult and arcane, was already comfortable on her tongue.

Harold vaguely recalled his wife's account of a magazine article about a girl who had simply stopped eating and starved herself to death, but he couldn't remember the particulars. He had little faith in the press in general and the articles Grace quoted in particular, and in this case the subject matter had been so unpleasant and, given Francesca's recent behavior, so ominous, that Harold had quickly pushed it from his mind.

"Maybe you better refresh my memory about it," he said.

Grace tried to put together what she remembered of the article with the information Dr. Gordon had given her this afternoon in a way that would not anger Harold. "Well, to begin with, it's a disease that strikes young girls, young girls from good families. They begin to diet, and then they won't stop or can't stop and it gets worse and worse."

"It's this damn fashion thing. A bunch of fag fashion designers tell women they're supposed to look like men—not even like men, like flagpoles—and women all over the world start dieting their asses off."

"According to Dr. Gordon, no one really knows what causes it. That's what the article said too. It admitted that this fashion business contributes to it. Society keeps telling women they have to be skinny to be attractive."

Harold was surprised. One of the reasons he paid so little attention to the articles Grace quoted so liberally was that they rarely agreed with his own theories.

"Dr. Gordon said it might have something to do with girls being afraid to grow up. They think if they go on looking like little girls, they can go on being little girls. They're afraid to be women, so they're afraid to look like women."

"You mean they're afraid of sex."

"I don't think that's the point, although if I remember correctly, that article said there were some doctors who blame it on that. But I got the impression that it was less being afraid of sex than being afraid of being adults."

"It sounds kind of crazy to me."

"I guess that's the point, Harold. It is kind of crazy. Dr. Gordon said one theory is that it has something to do with a brain lesion. Something goes wrong with the part of the brain that controls the appetite."

"I don't understand, Grace. You told me two weeks ago that Dr. Gordon said there was nothing physically wrong with Francesca. Now you're telling me she's got some kind of brain damage."

"I didn't say Francesca has brain damage. Dr. Gordon doesn't think that theory holds up either. In fact, she didn't really give me any explanation of what causes this anorexia."

"Terrific! You and that crazy woman sit around discussing medical theories, but when it comes to what's wrong with my daughter, no one has any answers."

"What you want, Harold, are simple answers, and I don't think there are any in this case." Grace stopped for a moment as if gathering strength for the battle ahead. "Dr. Gordon thinks Francesca ought to see a psychiatrist."

"A psychiatrist! Francesca's not crazy."

"I don't think crazy is a reasonable word to use,

Hal. Our daughter's disturbed about something, and Dr. Gordon thinks she needs professional help."

"Professional help. What in hell are we? Amateurs? We've raised three kids, damn nice kids, if you ask me." For the moment Harold seemed to have forgotten his dissatisfaction with Susanna. "And that qualifies us as professionals just as much as some shrink with a lot of diplomas and a Park Avenue office."

"Dr. Gordon gave me two names, Harold. Only one is on Park Avenue. The other is on Eighty-seventh Street."

"All right, Grace, maybe I did fly off the handle, but the idea of taking Francesca to a shrink just makes me mad. She's always been such a good kid. I can't believe all of a sudden there's something screwed up about her."

"Well, apparently there is, Harold. All you have to do is take a look at her or watch her eat or . . ."—Grace remembered their argument this afternoon, and the frustration and the tears began to well up again—"or try to talk to her to know that."

Hal's anger dissolved in the new flood of tears, and he put his arm around his wife. "I'm sorry, Grace. If Francesca needs a psychiatrist, we'll see that she gets a psychiatrist. How do we go about making an appointment?" When there were practical matters at hand, Hal could always take command. "Does Dr. Gordon set one up or do you want me to call?"

"We have to call. I'll do it if you don't want to."

"No, I'll do it. Which one do you want me to call?"

"I don't know. Dr. Gordon didn't recommend one over the other."

"Well, then why don't we call the first name? What is it?"

"Smith. Dr. Alexander Smith."

Harold began to laugh. It was more a release from tension than a reflection of any humor he saw in the situation. "Smith! What kind of shrink is named Smith? It's a ripoff, you know. I mean we ought to get a name like Freud or Krunnstaat or even Schmidt for our money, but Smith . . . well, at least it's not Keigelfaven. Remember Professor Keigelfaven on the old Sid Caesar Show, Grace? Remember the way he used to crack me up? Well, let's just hope Smith isn't as crazy as old Keigelfaven. Let's just hope Smith can put Francesca back together again." The moment of humor had passed, and Harold was face to face with the problem again, the problem that all of his courage and intelligence and hard work could not solve. "How long did Dr. Gordon say this was going to take? I mean, how long before she starts to get better?"

"Dr. Gordon didn't say, and to tell you the truth, Harold, I don't think she knows. It isn't like an operation or anything like that. You can't say she'll be up in two days or a week or a month."

6

"I know that, Grace." He was impatient again. Sometimes it seemed that Grace tried to make him sound like a fool. "But it seems to me she could give us a rough idea, at least in terms of years. I mean, sometimes these things go on forever. Our accountant, Al Geller, he's got a son who's twenty-five years old. The kid—and obviously he's not a kid anymore—has been seeing a shrink for ten years. That's all he does now—according to Geller—see a shrink and lie around the house feeling sorry for himself. I don't want to see that happening to Francesca. And to be perfectly honest, I have no intention of supporting a shrink for the next ten years. Don't get me wrong, Grace," he went on quickly. "I've always tried to give the kids everything. A nice home. The best schools. Everything. And I'll spend as much money as we have to to get Francesca well—*if* she's getting well—but I'll be damned if I'll pay some shrink fifty dollars an hour for the next ten years to help my daughter starve herself to death."

"Why don't we worry about that after we've seen the doctor, Hal? In the meantime, all we can do is call him and set up an appointment. After we see

77

him, and more important, after he's seen Francesca, we can begin to worry about how long this might or might not take."

It was a simple phone call, Hal told himself, a simple phone call like a hundred others he made every day. But as he sat in his office and stared at the old-fashioned black telephone, he knew it wasn't simple at all, and it was nothing like those daily calls he made with such ease. He wasn't calling a supplier or an account. He was calling a psychiatrist, a man who treated crazy people, and he was calling him to treat his own daughter. Even when Susanna was at her most difficult, they had never thought she needed "professional help." Discipline, yes, but a psychiatrist, no. But now Francesca, his baby, his good little girl who had never given him a moment's worry, needed one.

Hal got up and paced across his office a few times. Then he lit a cigar and stood looking out the grime-streaked window at his own particular view of the West Side. It wasn't a pretty view, he knew, but it was a familiar one, and he enjoyed it as much now as when it was new and he'd stood in front of it telling himself that he'd done it. He had his own business, and he'd make it work.

He stopped himself short. This wasn't the time for reminiscing. He had told Grace he'd call the psychiatrist, and by God, he'd call the psychiatrist. And he wasn't going to be intimidated by him, either. He pressed the intercom and barked into it. "Get me Dr. Smith, Maria. Dr. Alexander Smith, 289-1747."

Harold picked up the phone before the intercom ceased buzzing. "Dr. Smith's with a patient, Mr. Dietrich. Do you want to talk to his secretary?"

78

"No, Maria, no secretaries. I want to talk to Dr. Smith."

The girl got off again, then was back in a moment. "He'll return your call when he's free. Probably at ten of the hour."

Ten of the hour. The phrase rankled Harold. You paid fifty bucks for an hour, and all you got was fifty minutes. What a racket.

By the time Dr. Smith called back, Harold had worked himself into a minor rage at the whole situation, but it was hard to maintain anger in the face of this carefully modulated voice. Harold was accustomed to hail-fellow-well-met salesmen and deferential secretaries and even irate accounts, but there was something unreal about this calm, flat voice. The accent was good, but emotion, even feigned emotion, was lacking.

Harold listed the pertinent information quickly —Dr. Gordon, his daughter, something called anorexia nervosa. He was surprised at the way the doctor reacted to the information. Hal had been convinced that his daughter had a rare disease, so rare that it might even be a figment of Dr. Gordon's imagination, but Dr. Smith seemed to take it as a matter of course. Hal remembered the article Grace had told him about. He was surprised and a little reassured to think there was a whole body of knowledge on this peculiar disorder he hadn't heard of till less than a month ago.

"I can see you and your wife and daughter on Thursday at one."

"An evening appointment would be more convenient."

"I don't have evening appointments, Mr. Dietrich." There was no arrogance in the voice, only the same matter-of-fact flatness.

Harold thought of Francesca and subdued his anger. "Okay, one o'clock on Thursday." He'd have to cancel a business lunch, they'd have to get Francesca out of school, but Dr. Smith's will would be done. He'd better be good, Hal thought. He'd better be damn good.

7

On Thursday three members of the Dietrich family approached the office of Dr. Alexander Smith on Park Avenue at Ninety-sixth Street with a variety of feelings. Grace, heading crosstown in a taxi, felt more optimistic than she had in weeks. Dr. Gordon had diagnosed the problem. Now Dr. Smith would treat it. Grace had never admitted it to Harold, but she had great respect for psychiatry. It seemed to her that if more people sat down and talked things out calmly and clearly, there would be fewer problems in the world. Ideally, one should be able to talk things out with members of the family, as she and Susanna often did, or at least with a friend; but failing that, a psychiatrist was the next best thing. And Grace was sufficiently informed to realize that in certain instances, especially emotion-charged instances such as this one, a psychiatrist was better than someone closer. He could be more objective. A psychiatrist had no vested interest. Except in his fee, Harold would say, but Grace was feeling too hopeful today to let her husband's skepticism get to her.

Sixty blocks south in another taxi, Harold was not nearly so optimistic. The shrink wanted to see all three of them. Did that mean that he blamed whatever was wrong with Francesca on them? That's what these guys usually did. People got divorced because they hated their mothers. Children turned out bad because of their toilet training. Francesca was sick because sometime, somewhere, they had done something to her. Hal wondered how far back they stretched the line. If he was a bad father, a bad person, then it must be the result of his own childhood, his own parents. Hal began to prepare himself for a battery of questions about his life, and as he did, he began to get angry. He wasn't going to talk about his sex life. It was nobody's damn business what he did or didn't do. That was a private matter that had nothing to do with Francesca. The very idea that it might infuriated him, and he was already preparing the curt answer that would cut Dr. Alexander Smith and his prying questions short.

Walking up Madison Avenue toward the doctor's office, Kessa felt neither optimism nor anger. Her only emotion was fear. She must protect Kessa at all costs. She'd lie as much as necessary, but the doctor must not find out about Kessa and all the important habits and practices that kept her alive.

Next to the door was a brass plate. *Alexander Smith, M. D.* Harold ran his finger over the lettering. Nice machine work. The thought of the good work and his own appreciation of it gave him courage. He pressed the bell and waited until he heard the click of the latch. Neither Grace nor Francesca had arrived, and the waiting room was empty. It was furnished carefully in what Harold supposed was meant to be a restful style, with reproductions of Queen Anne and Duncan Phyfe and all the rest.

The black shades on the two brass lamps kept the lighting to a minimum. Harold picked up a copy of *Newsweek*, but when he found he could read only by holding it directly under the circle of light, he tossed it aside. He examined the furniture again, picturing Dr. Smith's wife choosing it. Then he heard the buzzer and the latch, and Grace was in the waiting room.

"What kept you?"

"Nothing kept me, Hal. I'm not late."

Harold checked his watch. He'd been earlier than he'd thought.

"Where's Francesca?" he asked.

"She didn't want me to pick her up. Said she'd rather come on her own."

"Just as long as she does come."

"She'll be here," Grace said with more assurance than she felt; but the buzzer proved her right. "Why don't you sit over there, Francesca?" Grace indicated the chair next to hers. Without looking at it, Kessa walked to the other side of the room and sat in a corner.

"This isn't going to do anyone any good if you're not cooperative, Francesca." But Harold's lecture was cut short by the appearance of a middle-aged man in a business suit. Harold stood, but the man walked past him and out of the office. Hal sat again, feeling sheepish. "I thought that was Dr. Smith."

"So did I," Grace reassured him.

"Average-looking guy. I wonder what he needs a shrink for?" Hal was cut short again by the appearance of the real Dr. Smith. He stood in the doorway to the inner office, tall and lean, with very short fair hair and clean features.

"Will you come in, please." The accent was impeccable, and Hal drew himself up to his full height. Still, he felt like an immigrant.

There were two chairs in front of the huge mahogany desk, both considerably smaller than the high-backed one behind it. Dr. Smith drew up a third for Francesca. Then he introduced himself and shook hands with each of them.

"How old are you, Francesca?" Dr. Smith asked, pencil poised above a yellow legal pad.

Kessa said nothing. "Fifteen," Grace replied.

"And what seems to be the problem?"

Still no sound from Kessa.

"The problem is," Harold said impatiently, "that she won't eat. Exactly what I told you on the phone."

"Is that true, Francesca?"

Kessa sat small and sullen in the big chair, her eyes riveted on the floor.

"I think I'll have a word alone with Francesca," Dr. Smith said to her parents. "Then I'd like to see you both again."

"Your parents seem concerned about your weight," he continued when Hal and Grace had left the room. She did not respond. "Are you concerned about your weight?" Kessa said nothing.

Dr. Alexander Smith, however, was not so easily put off. His training had prepared him to deal with resistant patients. He had only to wait them out. The five minutes of silence that followed were child's play to Dr. Smith—and agony to Kessa. She did not dare lift her eyes from the floor, but she knew that Dr. Smith's had never left her. What was he looking for? Could he see Kessa? The thought was alarming. She hadn't planned to talk to him, but if words would protect Kessa, she was prepared to find them.

"Is this what it's like?"

"What what's like, Francesca?"

"I mean, am I supposed to come here and just sit?"

"If you want to." For the next few minutes she seemed to want to, but Dr. Smith would not relinquish his initial advantage. She hadn't answered his questions at first, but she had finally spoken.

"Where do you go to school, Francesca?" She told him. "Do you like it?"

"It's okay."

"Just okay?"

"What do you mean?"

"I mean, are there some things you like about it and some you don't? What about friends?"

"What about them?"

"Do you have any?"

Kessa shrugged. He was getting too close to home again.

"What about the teachers?"

For a moment Kessa thought of telling him about Madame but then decided against it. If he found out about Madame, he might find out about Kessa, and she couldn't take that chance.

"Well, Francesca," Dr. Smith said after another period of silence. "You can send your parents in now. And I'll see you next Tuesday at four. We'll see each other Tuesdays and Thursdays at four."

Grace and Hal looked up eagerly when she entered the waiting room, but Kessa returned to the chair in the corner without looking at them. "I guess it's our turn," Hal said gruffly, and he held the door open for his wife.

"You said over the telephone, Mr. Dietrich, that Dr. Gordon diagnosed Francesca's problem as anorexia nervosa?" Hal nodded impatiently. What kind of doctor was he that he had to ask a layman questions about diagnoses? "How tall is your daughter?"

Hal looked blank.

"Five feet four inches, a little more perhaps," Grace said.

"And what did she weigh before she stopped eating?"

"About ninety-eight."

"And what does she weigh now?"

"As of last week, on Dr. Gordon's scale, eighty-one."

"I see," Dr. Smith said, committing it all to his yellow legal pad.

Hal heard the pencil scratching against the paper in the heavy silences between questions and answers, and he wanted to scream. You *see!* Just what in hell *do* you see?

"How long would you say this has been going on, Mrs. Dietrich? When did you begin to notice the weight loss?"

The simple question, or rather the juxtaposition of the two questions, sent a wave of guilt over Grace. When had it started and when had she noticed it? Should she have picked up the signs before she did? If she had, would it have made any difference? "I can't say exactly when it started. I noticed Francesca was losing weight almost a month ago. We took her to Dr. Gordon, and by that time she was down to eighty-eight. She said she didn't want to look gross in a bikini," Grace added helplessly.

"What about other symptoms?" Dr. Smith continued to write while he talked. "Has she stopped menstruating?"

"Dr. Gordon said she missed her last period, but Francesca won't talk to me about it. She never has."

"Does she vomit a great deal? Induce vomiting, that is?"

It was clear from the look on both Grace and Harold's faces that the thought had never occurred to them. "I've never seen her," Grace said, "but she spends enough time in the bathroom." She was remembering the other peculiar bathroom behavior and wondering how she could bring it up. It seemed like the sort of thing a psychiatrist should know, but she couldn't just blurt it out.

"How does she eat?"

"Miserably," Hal said.

Dr. Smith raised his eyes from the legal pad and looked at Harold for a moment. "I mean, does she have any peculiar eating habits?" Grace went through the now familiar litany.

"And she's always complaining about her food," Hal added. "It's too hot or too cold, it doesn't taste right, she hates this, she hates that."

Dr. Smith wrote it all down on the pad. Scratch, scratch, scratch. He replaced the pencil in a pewter mug holding a dozen others and looked up. "Judging from what you've told me, I'd tend to agree with Dr. Gordon. It looks as if your daughter has anorexia nervosa."

We knew that before we came, Harold wanted to say. Instead he asked, "Can you help her?"

"That's hard to say, Mr. Dietrich. It's a serious problem, and to be perfectly honest with you, not

one we've had a great deal of success in treating."
Dr. Smith did not say, because he had no hard
evidence to prove it, that he did not believe the
disease was treatable. The girl would either learn to
live with her sickness—he might help her there—or
die of it. "Which is not to say she can't be helped.
I'd like to see her twice a week."

"For how long?"

"That's something we never know at the beginning of treatment, Mr. Dietrich. Perhaps a year,
perhaps two, perhaps four."

Hal looked the doctor straight in the eye. "And
what's your fee?"

Dr. Alexander Smith did not flinch. "Fifty dollars a session."

The calculator in Harold's brain worked quickly. Between five and twenty thousand dollars. Between five and twenty thousand dollars to get Francesca to eat. "It's an expensive problem."

"As I said before, Mr. Dietrich, it's a serious
problem. If, however, you feel you can't afford the
fee, there are clinics . . ."

"I can afford to pay my daughter's medical ex-
penses, Dr. Smith."

"Very well, then. I told Francesca I'd see
her next Tuesday at four. Her regular appointments
will be Tuesday and Thursday at four. If she misses
an appointment, you'll be billed anyway. I'll explain
that to Francesca next week."

"In other words, if my daughter cuts classes, I
still have to pay."

"Hal . . ." Grace interrupted.

"Mr. Dietrich, I don't think your hostility is
going to help matters. Now, there's one more thing
I'd like to discuss with you. The possibility of
hospitalization."

88

"Dr. Gordon said the point of going to you was to keep her out of the hospital," Harold said.

"That's our aim, of course, but as I said, there's no telling how the course of treatment in these things will go. It may take some time to break down your daughter's resistance, and if she continues to lose weight during that time, a hospital is the safest place for her. We can keep her under observation and prevent her from doing herself any more harm."

"Like starving herself to death?" Grace asked.

"Sometimes medical procedures such as intravenous feeding can be helpful in the short run, Mrs. Dietrich." Dr. Smith looked at his watch. "There's one final point I'd like to make clear. So long as Francesca is not in the hospital, so long as I'm treating her here in my office, all my communications will be with her. I will not report to either of you."

"Do you mean to say that if my wife or I call you to ask about Francesca, you won't talk to us?"

"What I mean, Mr. Dietrich, is that the relationship between doctor and patient, in this case between Francesca and me, is crucial and private. If I were to talk to you about what goes on in this office during her hour, I'd be betraying her trust, and that trust is very important to our work here. Francesca must feel that I am her doctor, not yours or Mrs. Dietrich's. Well, if that's clear . . . I'll expect to see Francesca next Tuesday at four."

Outside the office Harold looked at his watch. It was precisely ten minutes of two. "Prompt son of a bitch, isn't he?"

"Be reasonable, Harold. He's not going to be a better doctor, if he starts to run over and keeps other patients waiting."

"Why is it, Grace, that you're always so ready to see everyone else's point of view but mine?"

"Well, Francesca, what did you think of Dr. Smith?" Grace asked.

The girl shrugged her shoulders.

"How about some lunch?" Harold tried to sound more optimistic than he felt, but as he spoke he realized he had just come face to face with the problem again.

"I've got to get back to school," Kessa mumbled.

"Mother's expecting me this afternoon," Grace said.

"Okay, I'll grab something on my way back to the office." Harold hailed a cab. "Can I drop either of you?" Grace said she'd walk, and Kessa began moving down Park Avenue without bothering to answer her father.

"Twenty thousand dollars to get her to eat and teach her some manners," Harold grumbled to himself as he got into the cab.

It was a beautiful early spring day, the first after almost a week of rain, and Park Avenue looked clean and fresh in the April sunshine. Grace hated the weather and the well-dressed men and women and staring doormen. She hated everything cheerful that afternoon, and every Park Avenue mother whose daughter wasn't anorexic. She tried to console herself with the thought that these people had other problems, but there was no solace in the idea. What were bad marriages or rebellious children or financial setbacks compared to a daughter determined to starve herself to death?

Grace found herself examining every young girl she passed, measuring her against Francesca. She pictured other mothers observing her own daughter, wondering what was wrong with her, what had been done to her. It always came back to that. What had Grace done to her daughter, where had she failed her? If only being a mother were a job, like her brief teaching job of years ago or Harold's running of his business. But no, it was a position of trust, a moral test where one was graded by teachers, guidance counselors, doctors, psychiatrists, social workers, other mothers, grandmothers, and of course, ultimately fathers. Grace looked at a well-dressed woman crossing Park Avenue with assurance. Did all women feel they had to answer to their husbands for every move or mistake their children made? Did all women still feel bound by their mothers' judgments? She wasn't sure of the answer, but she did know that all women didn't have daughters who were anorexics. That was her honor.

She thought of how her mother would react when she told her about Francesca. After all, there was no point in trying to keep it from her—her mother could always tell when Grace was upset. She would sit there in her very precise way and stare at Grace until she told her. And then Grace's guilt would mount—for her failure as a mother and her failure as a daughter. When, Grace thought, would that ever stop? When would she stop comparing herself with her mother, with her mother's career? And when would Francesca begin to get better?

Kessa still hadn't caught her breath when she reached the street, but she had to get out of the studio. She could not bear to stay in the dressing room with the half dozen other girls who had just auditioned.

She began to walk quickly crosstown through the drizzle, but the images of the other girls dancing, leaping, turning followed her. *Kes-sa, Kes-sa, Kes-*

sa, she chanted as she walked. She'd done well; she was sure she had. Surreptitiously she ran her hand over her stomach. She was thinner than the other girls, so she must have been better. After all, wasn't the thinner the winner?

8

Kessa kept six appointments with Dr. Smith. At first they frightened her, then they amused her, finally they angered her. Despite the variety of her own reactions, the hours all followed a single pattern. Dr. Smith would ask her a question about school or her friends or her parents or even what she thought about losing weight. Sometimes Kessa would mumble a monosyllabic answer. Often she would say nothing. Whether she answered or not, the conversation would soon deteriorate into silence. She would sit staring at the rug. It was a deep purple oriental. Dr. Smith would sit staring at her. Once she discovered that he was going to do no more than stare at her, ask an occasional question, and wait for her to speak—my God, how he could wait for her to speak—she stopped fearing him and began to think what fools her parents were to waste their money this way. Then, on the sixth appointment, Dr. Smith showed that perhaps he was not such a fool after all. The day was uncommonly hot for early May, and he had turned on the air-conditioner. As Kessa sat staring at the floor and Dr. Smith sat staring at her, she began to shiver.

"Are you cold, Francesca?" She said nothing.

"Because if you are, I can turn off the air-conditioner." Still silence. "Do you know why you're cold, Francesca? You're cold because you've lost all your body fat. There's nothing left to keep you warm. That's why you're always cold lately."

It seemed that all those hours Dr. Smith had spent staring at Francesca he'd been watching Kessa after all. Kessa stood and walked out of his office. She swore she'd never return again.

That night after dinner, or rather after her parents had eaten dinner and Kessa had eaten a quarter of a piece of meatloaf and one of the four asparagus spears on her plate in time to her magic chant, she locked the door to her bedroom and started her daily examination. Lying on her back, running her hand over the sunken stretch of flesh that used to be her stomach, she discovered a patch of down. She was growing hair on her stomach, Her first response was panic. She raced to the bathroom, tore off her clothes, and stepped on the scale. Seventy-eight. She had not gained an ounce since yesterday. Kessa returned to her room to complete the nightly ritual. Hair on her stomach. Like fur. Soft and sleek and dark against her white skin. She remembered Dr. Smith's comments this afternoon. The hair would keep her warm. Who needed fatty tissue? Disgusting fatty tissue. Hair was warm and sleek and smooth. And it weighed nothing. She had planned to dance for two hours after dinner, but this new development in Kessa's body made her feel warm and secure and drowsy. Maybe she'd skip practice just this once. Kessa remembered too late to do anything about it now. She was weeks behind in the reading and she couldn't come up with another excuse. She'd exhausted her quota of those. The teachers had accepted her stories, but they no longer believed her fairy tales. She'd simply cut class. Then she wouldn't have to take the quiz or make up an excuse. She didn't really care.

Kessa ran a hand over the soft down on her stomach again, then turned on her side and curled into a neat warm ball. She fell asleep almost immediately.

The report was shocking. Grace looked at it in disbelief. Her straight-A daughter had gotten two C's and two failures. The note from the headmaster said he feared something was wrong with Francesca. Her teachers reported that she seemed preoccupied. She didn't listen, didn't turn in her homework, never volunteered in class. She had always been such a good student. The headmaster would be happy to meet with Mrs. Dietrich about the problem. And perhaps a professional consultation was in order for Francesca.

Francesca seemed uninterested. She had casually dropped her grades and the envelope from the headmaster on the kitchen table and left the room. When Grace followed her into her bedroom and demanded to know what these grades and this letter meant, Francesca merely sat with that flat, expressionless face Grace had wanted to slap more than once in the last few months.

"I'm asking you a question, Francesca. What is the meaning of this?"

Kessa smiled, but it was more a grimace than anything else. "I guess it means I'm just like Susanna." Then she went straight to the stereo, turned it on very loud, and began to dance. Grace stood and watched her for a few moments. She was shocked. The girl was so thin she seemed barely able to move, yet here she was whirling and jumping and leaping

95

as if she had all the energy in the world. Only once did Grace see her come down from a leap and sink a little as her left leg gave away. But Kessa, aware of her mother's presence, would not give in, and she caught her balance and kept dancing.

When Harold got home he found his wife sitting at the kitchen table staring with unseeing eyes at the papers before her. She pushed them across the table to him. "Damn," he muttered. "Damn." But there was no anger in his voice, only resignation. "One more expert who thinks we ought to get her professional help. A helluva lot of good it's done."

"Harold, remember when we first took her to Dr. Gordon, she said to watch what she eats and how much she exercises? Well, she won't tell me what she weighs, but I can tell she's still losing weight. And I saw her dancing this afternoon. She's like some kind of a whirling dervish. She looks as if she has all the energy in the world, but I don't think her legs are even strong enough to support her anymore. Do you think we ought to stop the dancing lessons?"

"Do you think it will do any good?"

"I wasn't thinking of it as a punishment. I just don't want her to hurt herself. Any more than she already has, I mean."

"Maybe I ought to call Dr. Smith."

"You know what he said."

"I know what he said, but I also know that Francesca's been going to him for two months now—incidentally that's eight hundred dollars' worth of professional help—and she hasn't gotten any better. In fact according to these school reports and what you've just said, she's getting worse. And I want to know why. I'm not going to ask him to betray his hallowed trust. I'm just going to ask him what's going on. Don't worry, Grace, I'll be polite about it. I'll ask the goddamn son of a bitch what the prognosis is. Is that polite enough for you?"

Hal recognized the carefully modulated tones and perfect accent. "I was just on my way out, Mr. Dietrich. Perhaps I could get back to you tomorrow."

"What I have to say won't take long, doctor. I'd just like to know how my daughter is doing."

"How she's doing?" Smith managed to make it sound like the most absurd question imaginable.

"That's right, how she's doing. She's been seeing you for two months. According to my wife, she's still losing weight, and according to her school, she has serious problems. As far as I can see, she's getting worse, not better. Now, I realize that's a layman's opinion"—Harold's voice was heavy with sarcasm—"and I was wondering what your opinion was. I was wondering how things looked to you after these two months of treatment."

"Well, to begin with, Mr. Dietrich, it hasn't actually been two months."

"Give or take a week," Harold said impatiently.

"What I meant was, Francesca hasn't kept her appointments for some time now."

"Hasn't kept her appointments?"

"I assumed you knew, Mr. Dietrich."

"How in hell would I know? I'm not the one in that office. If a kid plays hooky, Dr. Smith, it's the teacher who knows, not the parent. And it seems to me it's the teacher's responsibility to inform the parent."

"Well, I'm informing you now, Mr. Dietrich. Francesca has missed several appointments."

"How many is several?"

There was a silence, and Harold could picture Dr. Smith leafing through an expensive leather-bound calendar book. "The last time I saw her was April twenty-third."

"That was more than a month ago! More than six goddamn weeks ago."

"I understand your anger, Mr. Dietrich, but I don't think it's me you're angry at."

"You don't, do you. Well, I'll tell you something, you goddamn thief. It is you I'm angry at. Angry as hell at someone who forgets to mention that my daughter isn't showing up for appointments but doesn't forget to send the bills. Your second bill came two days ago, and it was for a whole month of appointments, a whole month of unkept appointments."

"I warned you about that at our first meeting, Mr. Dietrich."

"Well, now I'm going to warn you about something—a big fat malpractice suit." Harold heard the click and knew Dr. Smith had hung up on him.

"She hasn't been keeping her appointments?" Grace asked.

"Six goddamn weeks of appointments. And the no-good son-of-a-bitch just kept sending the bills."

"What are we going to do now?" The question, simple in its desperation, brought Harold back to the problem. He could get as angry as he wanted about Dr. Smith and the wasted money, but getting angry wasn't going to help Francesca. To judge from the last months, it seemed that nothing was going to help Francesca. But that was absurd. It couldn't be hopeless. Harold wouldn't let it be hopeless. He remembered the time back in '55 when he looked as if he'd never get through the winter. He was that close to bankruptcy. Well, he hadn't gone bankrupt. He'd fought back and built the business into what it was today. And if he could fight back for his business, he could sure as hell fight back for his kid.

"All right, Grace, I've had enough professional help. Now we're going to do this our own way. The first thing I'm going to do is talk to Francesca."

"It won't do any good to yell at her, Hal."

"I'm not going to yell at her. I'm going to talk to her as calmly as I'm talking to you now." And it was true, Grace noticed. Hal's fury of a few minutes ago had evaporated. He had decided to take things in his own hands, and when Harold was in control, he was never angry.

Locked in her room, lying flat on her back in her self-examining position, Kessa had heard her father shouting at Dr. Smith over the telephone. She thought she'd be frightened when he found out, but she wasn't frightened at all. She felt superior and removed and in control. Her father had lost control. He had screamed at the doctor and made a fool of himself. But Kessa hadn't lost control. She hadn't let the doctor get to her. She had simply stopped going to him, just as she had stopped doing other things that made her uncomfortable—like eating and sitting on the toilet seat and talking to her parents. And now she was in control of the situation and they were going to pieces because of her. Suddenly Kessa felt very powerful.

The feeling was shattered by the sound of her father's voice on the other side of the closed door. There was an unmistakable calmness to it, an authority that had nothing to do with his rage of a few minutes ago, and this new father was frightening. "Francesca, will you come out here please. I'd like to talk to you."

Kessa's mind raced. How could she ward him off? "Later," she called through the closed door. "I have a headache."

"I'd like to talk to you now, Francesca. It's important." Once again the calm authority.

"Let me just get an aspirin." She did not look at her father as she pushed past him toward the bathroom.

Slowly, methodically, she took the aspirin bottle from the medicine cabinet, took out two aspirins, swallowed one, drank half a glass of water, swallowed the other, finished the water, and washed her face. The ritual of it all was reassuring. The buzzing in her head stopped. She looked in the mirror. Francesca was gone. Kessa was in control. She walked into the living room. Her father was not sitting in his usual chair, but on the couch. She sat next to him. She did not look at him but could feel his eyes on her. She didn't want him to look at her. She wished she were invisible, wished she could shrink down into her stomach and disappear.

When he started to speak in that same controlled voice, the buzzing in her head began again. "I'm worried about you, Francesca. I'm worried about all this weight you've lost. I think something's bothering you, but I also think we can discuss it. Can you tell me what's bothering you, Francesca?"

He had leaned toward her as he spoke, and without meaning to, Kessa shrank back into the sofa. The buzzing grew louder, and she said nothing. It was important not to speak. Words would betray Kessa.

"I know we don't talk enough," her father continued. "I'm all wrapped up in my work and you're off in school or dance class, but I think we ought to try to talk more, Francesca. I think we ought to try to know each other better, and if something's troubling you, I'd like to hear about it. Perhaps I can even help."

His words were terrifying. He wanted to help. It was what she'd always wanted—Daddy helping, Daddy caring, Daddy—but now he seemed too dangerous to have. He had been too scary. Too threatening for too long. And even if this new, kinder Daddy lasted, she knew she couldn't go on having him. She'd be bound to lose him one way or another. It seemed safer not to risk having him at all. She said nothing and turned her body a little away from him.

Still calm, still in command, Hal decided to take a different tack. "Well if you won't tell me what's bothering you, Francesca, I'll tell you what's bothering me. All the weight you've lost. I'd like you to start eating again. I'd like you to start looking like the old Francesca again."

The old Francesca. She hated the old Francesca, a weak, frightened child who needed everyone and was never in control of herself or anyone else. "I don't want to look like the old Francesca. I like the way I look now. I like who I am now." She stopped abruptly. She'd almost gone too far.

"I don't understand, Francesca. Who are you now?"

She was silent again, and he returned to the more concrete argument, the one she had finally answered. "I don't think you can possibly like the way you are now. Just go look in the mirror, and you'll see that you're much too thin."

"I look in the mirror all the time, and I think I look just fine. I like the way I look."

"Well, I don't like the way you look. Neither does your mother and neither does Dr. Gordon.

Now, you may not care what we think, but you do care what we do, and I'll tell you what I've decided to do. First thing tomorrow morning I'm going to call Dr. Waldman and make an appointment for you."

"Who's Dr. Waldman?"

"A very good doctor I've known for a long time."

"But I just saw Dr. Gordon."

"Well, I don't think Dr. Gordon was strong enough in this case. I think maybe you need an old-fashioned male doctor. And just to make sure you keep the appointment, I'm going to take you myself. I'm not going to argue with you about Dr. Smith now; I didn't like him much myself, but you should have told us when you stopped keeping your appointments. However, I don't want to discuss that now. What I do want to discuss is the second thing I'm going to do. If you don't start eating, Francesca, if you don't begin to put on weight, I'm going to stop your dance classes."

"But you can't . . . especially not now, not just before the announcement of the audition results."

"I most certainly can. I'm your father, and I pay the bills, and I'm not going to pay to have you dance yourself into a skeleton. You have one week to change your habits. After that, dance class stops. I want you to know, Francesca, I'm not doing this to punish you. I'm doing it to protect you—from yourself. And one more thing. From now on I monitor your eating. You eat what I tell you to at dinner, and you don't leave the house in the morning till you've finished the breakfast I say you'll eat. Is that clear?"

Even if Kessa had wanted to answer, she couldn't have. The terror was choking her. It didn't matter how carefully she planned her meals now, how carefully she cut up the food or arranged it on the plate. She couldn't arrange anything, because her father was going to stand over her and force food into her.

Kessa sat staring at the far wall with unseeing eyes. Hal watched her. Had he been too harsh? Too weak? If only he could do something to cut through the wall that surrounded her. It seemed as if she didn't even hear him. It seemed as if she was not even there. Suddenly he wanted very much not to be there himself.

"I'm going to see what's for dinner," he said, and left the room.

When he entered the kitchen, Grace did not look up from the salad she was making. "How did it go?" she asked.

"Not very well." He noticed that her hands were shaking as she tore the lettuce to pieces. "I told her she has one week to start eating. If not, we stop dance class. I laid down a few other ground rules too."

"Such as?"

"She doesn't leave the table at night until she eats dinner to my satisfaction, and she doesn't leave the house in the morning until she's had a proper breakfast."

"Do you think it will work?"

"Someone's got to take a firm hand with her. So far all we've done is coddle and plead and drag her from one permissive doctor to another. Oh, that's the other thing. I'm going to make an appointment with Dr. Waldman. You remember Waldman. We knew each other as kids. Worked his way through college and med school, and there's nothing fancy or soft about him. Waldman's a good

103

old-fashioned GP. No fancy Park Avenue office and no specialties. Waldman doesn't treat an ear or a lung or a leg. He treats people. And I think that's what Francesca needs right now—someone to knock some sense into her."

"Maybe you're right . . ." Grace didn't really think so, but at this point she was ready to try anything.

"God, I hope so. Because if I'm not, I don't know what we're going to do." The despair in his voice made Grace look up, and she could read the same emotion in his eyes. Hal was revealing a side of himself he'd kept hidden for years, and Grace wasn't sure if she welcomed the glimpse into her husband or feared it.

9

For Kessa the next week passed as a nightmare, a nightmare of overwhelming terror in which her father played the brutal villain. He blocked the door and would not let her leave for dance class until she had finished a plate of scrambled eggs and bacon. He stood over her at dinner and directed her eating. "Now the potato, Francesca. You haven't touched your potato." One morning he even locked her in her room when she refused to eat the toast her mother had prepared. The fact that after almost every enforced meal she sneaked into the bathroom and threw it up kept Kessa from drowning in a sea of Francesca's fat, but it did not drive away the panic that haunted her days and made her nights restless and uneasy.

For the past months Kessa had kept herself in control by organizing carefully. Her days were consumed by arranging and rearranging the things in her room, by planning out her dance exercises, and most of all by plotting her meals. When would she next eat, what would she eat, how much, in what order? Would she eat one quarter of the meat or one third? Would she skip breakfast and eat a French fry or would she have exactly three bites of chocolate pudding. Kessa's body was starving for food, but her mind was drowning in it. Then her father took over, and everything was thrown out of kilter. No longer could she plan and plot and organize. She was out of control and she was terrified.

Harold had not misjudged his childhood friend Waldman. He was a doctor of the old school. The tiny waiting room of his office on West Seventy-fourth Street was crowded with worn leather furniture that had obviously been in use as long as he had been in practice. From the single window a noisy air-conditioner blew gusts of cool air into the room. Kessa wished she'd remembered to bring a sweater. Her T-shirt provided little protection against the cold drafts. There was neither a receptionist nor a nurse, and in a few minutes Dr. Waldman himself opened the door to the inner office. Kessa sat huddled in a corner while her father and the doctor exchanged greetings.

"Now, what seems to be wrong with the girl, Hal?" Dr. Waldman's tone was gruff but not unkind.

"She won't eat. It's that simple. And she's losing weight like crazy."

"You mean she's lost her appetite?"

"I mean she won't eat. Her pediatrician and some shrink we sent her to—the damnedest thief you ever saw—diagnosed it as anorexia nervosa."

Waldman had heard of the disease but had never come across it in a patient. His Upper West Side practice consisted mostly of the elderly, the black, and the Spanish-speaking. It was a busy practice but not a fashionable one.

"Well, let's take a look at you," he said to

106

Francesca. "Go into the little room off the office and take off everything but your underpants. There should be a gown in there." He turned back to Hal. "I'll talk to you after the examination."

When Waldman opened the gown to examine her, he was shocked at Kessa's appearance. Harold hadn't exaggerated. She looked like those pictures of inmates in a concentration camp.

"Well, there's nothing wrong with your chest or stomach," he said, closing the gown, "except that there isn't enough of either. Let's see what you weigh. Seventy-seven."

Through the examination and the weighing, Kessa had kept her eyes straight ahead, her face impassive, and Waldman was beginning to get angry with this kid who was willfully making herself ill. He thought of a patient he had seen less than two hours ago, a Puerto Rican girl just about this one's age. She was losing weight too, but in her case there was a reason for it. The child had leukemia. There was enough sickness and suffering in the world without this headstrong girl starving herself to death.

"How long do you think you can stay alive at that weight?" The bony shoulders shrugged, but the face was still impassive. Waldman's anger was building. "Well, I'll tell you. Not very long." He began to take her blood pressure and yanked her arm around roughly. "Your blood pressure's eighty over fifty. Normal blood pressure for you would be one-twenty over seventy. You don't know what that means, but I'm going to tell you what that means. It means that any moment you could drop dead from shock."

The control was gone, and Kessa was close to

tears now, more because of Dr. Waldman's tone than the words themselves. He noticed the change and didn't care what the reason for it was.

"But I have no intention of letting you drop dead from shock or any other result of this crazy dieting. If you keep this up, young lady, I am going to slap you right into a hospital. If you keep on refusing to eat, we'll hospitalize you and stick an IV into your arm and drip enough glucose into you to keep you alive and get some meat on your bones again. And if that doesn't work, we'll put a tube through your nose that runs down to your stomach. Do you think you'd be comfortable lying in a hospital bed with a tube running through your nose into your stomach?"

Kessa could barely hold back the tears now.

"Well, I can tell you, you wouldn't be in the least comfortable. But there's only one way you can keep me from doing that, and that's by starting to eat and putting on some weight. Is that perfectly clear? You're to stop all this dieting nonsense. Now you go get dressed while I tell your father exactly what I've told you. There isn't a thing wrong with you, but there will be if you don't start eating."

Harold entered the small office and took the worn chair in front of Waldman's desk. "I think I may have talked some sense into her, Hal. I threatened her with hospitalization, which incidentally is no empty threat. If her weight keeps dropping, it's the only way to keep her alive. But I don't think we'll have to resort to that. I took a firm hand, and I suggest you do the same at home. See that she eats."

"That's exactly what I've begun doing."

"Good. And weigh her every day. That way

you can keep track of what she's doing. You might give me a call in a couple of weeks."

In the cab on the way home Harold was pleased. He'd been right to take a firm hand, right to take her to a good old-fashioned GP like Waldman who could talk some sense into her. Enough of Dr. Smith and his "Well, we can't really say," "Well, we don't really know." Every time he thought of that goddamn shrink his blood began to boil. Well, he didn't have to think about him anymore. Francesca was in his hands now, his and Waldman's.

"What did you think of Dr. Waldman?"

"I thought he was disgusting! I thought he was a mean, disgusting man!" It was the longest and most impassioned response Hal had gotten from his daughter in weeks, but perhaps that was a good sign.

"Well, you don't have to like him to take his advice."

Kessa thought of the food that had come to terrorize her so. It wasn't only that she didn't want to eat more than those carefully determined portions. She couldn't eat more.

"And what if I can't take his advice?" she shot back.

"Now, that's the most ridiculous thing I've ever heard. Of course you can take Waldman's advice. He told you to start eating, and you can simply make up your mind to forget this foolish diet and start eating." When she said nothing, Hal went on. "And you might as well do it willingly, because if you don't I'm just going to keep forcing you to eat."

Harold continued to monitor his daughter's eating habits, but as the days passed and the scale continued to drop, his anger mounted. He stared across the dinner table at the pale skeleton who used to be his daughter. She was beating on the side of a dish of ice cream with her spoon. Tap, tap, it went. Tap, tap.

"Time for your nightly weigh-in, Francesca." The anger was barely veiled under the lighthearted words.

"You might at least wait till I finish dinner," she said. Tap, tap. Tap, tap.

The clicking noise broke through Harold's control. "Then eat your dinner, goddamn it, and stop that infernal tapping."

"How can I eat my dinner when you keep screaming at me?" Tap, tap. Tap, tap.

Harold grabbed his daughter's shoulder and wrenched her from the chair. "You can finish your dinner later," he barked as he began to push her toward the bathroom. Still holding her arm, he maneuvered her onto the scale. The dial stopped at seventy-five. Harold saw the number and wanted to slap her. Suddenly he remembered a question that Dr. Smith had asked him. What a fool he was! It had never occurred to him that Francesca would be throwing up the food he forced down her.

"Have you been making yourself vomit, Francesca?" She kept her eyes on the scale. The magic seventy-five seemed more important than her father's rage. "Answer me, have you been making yourself vomit?"

"I haven't been making myself. I can't help it if you force too much food into me and I can't keep it down."

"Too much food. You call one lamb chop and three string beans too much food?" He dragged her back down the hall to her room and threw her into
110

a chair. "I warned you, Francesca, but you wouldn't listen. As of tomorrow there will be no more dance class." He looked around the room in helpless anger. "And there will be no more stereo and no more TV and no more telephone. I've had enough of your damned craziness. I tried to reason with you, but you wouldn't let me. Well, if punishment is what you want, punishment is what you're going to get. You may refuse to eat, Francesca, but you're going to be one bored skeleton, I can tell you that."

He slammed the door behind him, and her sobbing stopped as suddenly as if it were a light that had been switched off. Her face contorted into a mask of hatred. She made a grotesque grimace at the door—at him. She sat staring at the door in hatred, thinking without really thinking of all the doors she had made faces at over all the years because she was too frightened of him or her or them and a door seemed so much safer.

10

Kessa walked across Fifty-third Street thinking of Madame's response to the news that she would no longer be attending class. The teacher hadn't seemed to care at all. *Perhaps it was because I didn't do well at the audition for the summer sessions.* Kessa hadn't thought she'd done badly. She'd been frightened, but her rituals had gotten her through —though apparently they hadn't gotten her through well enough. Two weeks after the audition, Madame had informed her that although she'd done fairly well, she hadn't qualified for the summer session. Madame had not added that the judges found Kessa technically sufficient but stiff and lacking in grace. Strangely, Kessa hadn't felt as bad about not being chosen as she'd expected to. It was like Madame's response today. *She sure didn't seem to care much that I was leaving. I should feel sad.* For a while Kessa concentrated on feeling sad, but she couldn't seem to summon up any emotion. *Maybe I can't feel anything anymore. Anyway I'd rather not dance than be fat.* She was passing a coffee shop, and there was a menu in the window. It was late afternoon and she ought to be getting home, but she merely stood in front of the coffee shop window reading the menu over and over again, adding calories, adding prices, dividing them, turning the menu into a magical puzzle that she had to solve.

Hal had relinquished control and slid back into the old pattern of alternating inattention and outbursts of temper. Gratefully Kessa returned to her old routine. Her room was in perfect order. Her visits to the bathroom and her behavior once there were carefully planned. She spent most of the day thinking out what she would eat and how. The evenings were given over to examinations of her body.

She lay on her back and walked her fingers down her ribs, skipped them over her abdomen, and landed on her pelvic bones. She tapped them with her knuckles. The room was silent—her father had made good his threats—and she could hear the sound of knuckle against bone. *I can hear my bones*, she thought. Her fingers moved up from her pelvic bones to her waist. The elastic of her underpants barely touched the center of her abdomen. *The bridge is almost finished*, she thought. The elastic hung loosely around each thigh. More progress. She put her knees together and raised them in the air. No matter how tightly she pressed them together, her thighs did not touch. "Bravo," she murmured, much as Madame used to when she had executed a step well in class.

Kessa ran her hands over her body again. The hair was getting thicker. That must be a good sign. Her body was healthy. Her body was taking care of itself. So much for her parents and the doctors and all their terrible warnings. Her body could take care of itself.

Kessa was so lost in the pleasure of her own examination that she hadn't heard the knock at the door, and then it was too late and her mother was standing at the end of the bed. Kessa could read the horror in her face. Grace had not seen her daughter in only her underpants for more than a month. *Well, she can be as horrified as she wants,* Kessa thought. *I like the way I look.*

Grace had been shocked the last time she had walked in on her daughter, but that had been nothing compared to her appearance now. Suddenly the months of worry erupted in a volcano of rage. "You're crazy," she shrieked. "Look at what you've done to yourself. You're absolutely crazy. What do you weigh now?"

Kessa merely shrugged the thin-shouldered dismissal that had begun to drive Grace mad.

"Well, we're going to find out what you weigh," she screamed, dragging Kessa from the bed and repeating Hal's procedure of the weeks before; but this time the evidence was most alarming. She'd lost two more pounds. A picture of the models she'd cut out of the magazine flashed through Kessa's mind. *And the winner is . . . seventy-three!*

At a few minutes after nine the next morning, Grace called Dr. Gordon. Her voice heavy with despair, she catalogued the failures of the last months. Dr. Smith and the unkept appointments. Hal's assumption of control and relinquishing of it. Her own alternating spurts of helplessness and rage. And through it all Francesca just kept losing weight —moving further and further away from them and losing more and more weight.

Evelyn Gordon listened with a sinking feeling. She had been treating Francesca Dietrich since she was born, and now it seemed certain that

115

Francesca Dietrich was going to die, and there was nothing she could do but stand by and watch. When she spoke, however, her voice was efficient and matter-of-fact. "The first thing I want you to do, Mrs. Dietrich, is bring Francesca in for another examination. We'll have to consider hospitalization, I'm afraid."

Dr. Gordon hesitated for a moment, turning something over in her mind. She knew that after the incident with Dr. Smith any psychiatrist she might recommend would be suspect, but she was remembering a young man she'd met at a dinner party several nights ago. It had been one of those typical medical evenings where the talk revolved around new procedures, the high cost of malpractice insurance, and the latest book or paper by so-and-so. The young man—not so young, Evelyn corrected herself; he must be well into his thirties—was a psychologist, and his lack of a medical degree made him something of an outsider.

"I imagine a lot of this is pretty boring for you," she'd said when they had moved to the living room for coffee and brandy and she'd found herself next to him.

"No more so than any group of professionals. People talk about what interests them."

"And in your case, what's that?" she asked. "I mean, what sort of a practice do you have?"

"A beginning one," he'd laughed, but then, seeing that her interest was genuine, he'd gone on. He hadn't been able to shake his last patient of the day and was grateful to be able to talk about it. "I'm treating an anorexic now. Actually two of them and . . ." He'd let his voice trail off. And what? Could he say to this strange woman that he was frightened, frightened that he might lose the

116

girl, frightened that she was beginning to take over too much of his life?

"They're not easy," Evelyn had said. "I'm surprised you're treating two of them. Most psychiatrists hate to take them on. I imagine you've heard the arguments—uncooperative, sneaky, dishonest. I suspect what it really amounts to is that they're not very likable girls—oh, they may have been originally, but they're not by the time the disease is recognizable—and I think it troubles most psychiatrists to admit to themselves that they simply don't like a patient. It's easier not to treat them."

"Easier for the doctor, at any rate."

"Well, I wish you luck. Have you had any so far?"

"No miracle cures, but some success. The first one has stayed out of the hospital now for a year. In her case that's a record. Before this she'd been in and out every couple of months for the last three years."

Evelyn was impressed. He was right. It was no miracle cure, but it was a good sign.

She hadn't put the psychologist together with Francesca Dietrich because she'd assumed the girl was still seeing Dr. Smith. After that debacle she only hoped she could convince the Dietrichs to venture into psychiatry a second time.

"There's something else I'd like to try, Mrs. Dietrich. There's a psychologist who's been treating some of these anorexic girls. Now I'm not promising you he can cure Francesca, but I was impressed by some of the results he reported. I think we ought to give him a try."

"Dr. Gordon, at this point I'll try anything."

"Fine. I'll see you and Francesca tomorrow at three, and by that time I ought to have something set up with this psychologist. His name is Sherman, Sandy Sherman."

"Well, at least," Hal said when Grace reported the conversation to him, "it beats Smith."

Grace sat in the waiting room of Evelyn Gordon's office with an unopened copy of *New York* magazine on her lap. She was too nervous to read. It was three-fifteen and Francesca had still not arrived. After lunch—if you could call the spoonful of cottage cheese and two melon balls Francesca ate lunch—she'd said she wanted to go for a walk. "Now that you don't let me dance anymore, I never get any exercise." Grace had worried about her daughter's being on time for the appointment with Dr. Gordon, but since Francesca had shown no desire to leave the apartment since Harold had stopped her dance classes, she'd reasoned that the walk was a good sign.

"Just make sure you're at Dr. Gordon's office by three. I'll meet you there."

Kessa hadn't planned not to show up, but neither had she been prepared for the obstacles the city had thrown in her path on this steamy July day. At first she'd thought she'd walk in the park, but two hot-dog carts and an ice-cream wagon blocked her path. She stood on the corner staring at them unable to move. She thought about hot dogs. One hundred twenty-four calories. Divide the hot dog into four pieces, four exactly equal pieces. Thirty-one calories. And what if you sliced that into another four pieces, four tiny symmetrical discs of seven and three-fourths calories each? Kessa's stomach rumbled, and she felt dizzy with wanting a hot dog, a quarter of a hot dog, a sixteenth of a hot dog. Fewer than eight calories. Then she remembered lunch. The mound of cottage cheese. She never

118

should have had so much. It must have been at least a hundred calories. The cottage cheese plus the melon plus the iced tea plus the quarter of a hot dog . . . As she stood there doing additions in her head, two girls eating ice-cream popsicles walked by. The coating glistened wetly the way icy chocolate does in the heat. The sight of it made Kessa cold despite the hot breeze coming off the park.

She had to get away from the park, from the army of food vendors swarming around her. She began to walk down Central Park West. Her hunger —and the endless computations of breakfast and lunch and breakfast and lunch and hot dog and hot dog divided by two, four, sixteen—made her tired, but she kept up a brisk pace. It was good exercise, she told herself. Each time she saw a hot-dog wagon or an ice-cream cart, she crossed to the other side of the street. At the corner of Seventy-fourth Street, Kessa had stared so hard at the man with the Good Humor wagon that he'd asked her what it would be. She began to run to the other side of the street, and a taxi swerved, narrowly missing her.

"Crazy kid," the driver yelled out the window.

Halfway down \Seventy-second Street, Kessa realized she had trapped herself. Fleeing the nightmare of food that filled the park and lined Central Park West, she had turned onto this thoroughfare of bakeries and delis, pizza stands and ice-cream parlors, and small groceries smelling of barbecued chickens. A piece of barbecued chicken. Two hundred ten calories. She was walking faster now, almost running. The smells were coming fast, one after another, and Kessa was calculating. Could she have this? No, a bagel was too much. How about that? A child's ice pop steaming in the afternoon heat.

Maybe half an ice pop. Only seventy-five calories. But still too many calories. Damn Kessa for putting butter on that half piece of toast this morning. She remembered the butter melting on the crunchy piece of bread, and she felt dizzy with fear. Her T-shirt was wet and stuck to her back and ribs. The sweat was pouring down her sides. It felt as if something were creeping down her body. She stopped at the corner and looked up at the street signs. She had to get her bearings. She had to get control of herself. Kessa took several deep breaths. She would eat nothing. Not a bagel, not an ice pop, nothing. Good, clean, pure nothing. She breathed deeply again. That was better. Kessa was in control.

She started walking back toward Central Park West and remembered the appointment with Dr. Gordon. She looked at her watch, the band hanging loosely around her wrist. Three-thirty. What time was her appointment? She couldn't remember. Her mother had told her, but Kessa had been concentrating on the cottage cheese when she mentioned it. She hailed a cab going east. It was three forty-five when she entered Dr. Gordon's waiting room.

"Where have you been?" Grace demanded. That shrug again. "You're forty-five minutes late. Do you think you're Dr. Gordon's only appointment?"

"The doctor will squeeze you in now," the receptionist interrupted.

"We were beginning to worry about you," Dr. Gordon said when Kessa was undressed and sitting on the examining table.

For a moment the old polite Francesca surfaced. "I'm sorry, I lost track of the time."

"Well, you're here now. Let's see what kind of condition you're in." Evelyn Gordon needed no in-

120

struments to see what kind of condition the girl was in, but she proceeded with her examination, saving the scale for last. "Hop on, Francesca." Far from hopping, Kessa approached the scale as a prisoner does the guillotine. The competent hands slid the weights down, down, down. "Seventy-three." There was a moment of silence. "Sit down, Francesca."

Kessa sat on the chair next to the examining table and pulled the gown closer around her. The air conditioning was freezing.

"Look at me, Francesca." Kessa raised her eyes slowly, unwillingly. Dr. Gordon's own were stern. "I'm not going to plead or argue anymore; I'm simply going to tell you. You're dangerously underweight. If you lose any more weight, I'm going to put you right in the hospital. I'd put you in today . . ."

Kessa's head started to buzz. Today. They couldn't put her into the hospital today. They couldn't!

". . . but I'm eager for you to see a Dr. Sherman your mother and I have discussed. But I'm going to keep in touch with him—no skipped appointments this time, Francesca—and I'm going to see you once a week. That means a week from today. And I warn you Francesca, if you've lost any more weight, you'll be in the hospital by that night."

Kessa heard the words and shut them out. They had been threatening her with the hospital for months now. All of them. But she was still free. She had outwitted her father and her mother, and Dr. Gordon and Dr. Smith and Dr. Waldman. Kessa had outsmarted them all. Now she started to worry about this Sherman character.

11

Kessa went alone to Sherman's office. "If the appointment is for me, I don't see why you have to tag along," she told her mother. "After all, you're not the one that everyone's picking on."

"No one is picking on you, Francesca. We're trying to help you."

"Some help. Every other day you threaten to throw me into the hospital."

The accusation stung. Grace had noticed that Harold had begun to threaten Kessa with hospitalization as one threatens a small child with a spanking. And Grace supposed her own behavior was similar, even if her motives were different. Every time she sat across a table from her daughter watching her pick at her food, every time she got a glimpse of the bones protruding through the thin fabric of her summer clothes, every time she scraped a full plate into the trash, Grace felt a stab of fear for her daughter's life. "You know what Dr. Gordon said," she warned again and again, but what she was really saying was "I wish they'd put you in the hospital; I wish they'd save you from yourself and your craziness before it's too late."

"Well, anyway, it's my doctor and my hour and I don't need you along," Kessa said.

Grace remembered Dr. Smith, the unkept appointments, and the forty-five minute wait at Dr. Gordon's, but she decided to go along with Francesca's demand. Maybe it was a good sign. Maybe Francesca had decided to take her health into her own hands.

The self-service elevator was tiny and rickety. Like a cell, Kessa thought.

Please Ring Bell and Walk In, the sign at the side of the door said. The small room was empty. It reminded her of Dr. Waldman's waiting room, only it wasn't depressing. The furniture was worn and the magazines had that limp, wrinkled waiting-room look, but the office didn't seem like Dr. Waldman's. She decided it was because of the pictures on the wall. They were brightly colored renditions of young girls and pleasant events. Dr. Waldman had some corny Norman Rockwell prints and a still life. Kessa remembered the bowl of oranges and bananas and realized she hadn't thought of food for at least an hour. She had been too busy worrying about Sherman.

A door to an inner office opened, and a girl about Kessa's age walked out. They eyed each other hostilely. Kessa had heard the casual "bye" the girl tossed over her shoulder. She both resented and envied it.

The door opened again and a man came out, Kessa had supposed he would be about the same age as Dr. Smith, that is, not as old as her father, but old. Somehow this Sherman looked younger. Kessa thought it might be the white jeans and the shirt without a jacket. But he wore a tie, she noticed.

Probably a fake, she decided. Trying to seem "with it." She supposed that was what the beard was for.

"Hi, I'm Sandy Sherman. You're Francesca Dietrich?" She nodded. "Come in." He indicated the inner office. It was bigger than the waiting room but as crowded. There were chairs and couches everywhere.

"Have a seat." Something was wrong. She could feel it. He was too casual.

"Where?"

"Wherever you like."

Kessa stood frozen in the center of the room. He walked to one corner and sat down. She sat opposite him but kept her eyes on the carpet.

"What can I do for you?" His voice was still casual, as if she had wandered into a store and he was offering to wait on her. Either a phony or a fool, she decided.

"What do you mean . . . Dr. Sherman," she added, to show him he might as well cut the crap. She knew he was a shrink.

"Well, to begin with, Francesca, most people call me Sandy."

"Sandy?"

"That's right. What do most people call you?"

"Kessa." It came out without a moment's hesitation.

"Well, Kessa, people who come to see me usually have some sort of problem they want to straighten out. I assume you do too, and since nobody else told me about it, I guess you'll have to."

She was suspicious again. "You mean Dr. Gordon and my mother didn't tell you what was wrong?"

"Dr. Gordon gave me a physical report over

the phone, Kessa, but I'm not a physical doctor. She takes care of that part of you. So why don't you tell me about the other part? Why don't you tell me what your problem is?"

"I don't have a problem; they do. They think I'm losing too much weight."

"Who's they?"

"Everybody, but mostly my parents."

"So you're here because your parents think you're losing too much weight?"

She nodded.

"Now I know what your parents want from me, but I don't know what you want. I mean, if you decide to come here and talk to me, what do you want out of it?"

She was confused. No one had ever asked her anything like that before. She had no answer and tried to distract herself by taking off her sweater. She saw his eyes go to her arms, the beautiful bones and soft down.

"I guess you have lost weight," he said. She sat staring at the floor waiting for the usual lecture to follow, but he said nothing. His silences were more disconcerting that Dr. Smith's.

"I don't know what you want me to say."

"I don't want you to say anything, Kessa. Or rather, I want you to say whatever you feel like saying. But you don't have to say anything in particular to please me. Would you like me to get to know you, Kessa?" Sherman continued without missing a beat.

It was a frightening thought, but one he was forcing her to consider. "I don't know."

"Well, if you decide to see me on a regular basis, it means you do."

126

"Why?"

"Because if you begin coming on a regular basis, it means you have a problem you'd like help with. Not your parents, but you. And I believe the only way I can help you with that problem is by getting to know you very well."

Kessa looked at him suspiciously. She was surprised at his words, but she couldn't find anything really wrong with them.

"That's going to mean invading your privacy sometimes. I'm going to want to know what you do and what you think and everything about you. I'm going to want to understand everything you go through. It's the only way I'm going to be able to deal with whatever's bothering you."

The words were terrible, terrible and frightening, but his voice was so calm and matter-of-fact that it seemed to remove all the danger. Still, she felt some protest was in order. "I can't see why you'd want to know all that."

"For two reasons, Kessa. To begin with, if you share your thoughts with me, if we sit here and talk about them, you won't be so afraid of them." She was skeptical but said nothing "The other reason is that if you start to share your thoughts and feelings and fears with me, you won't feel so alone. You won't feel so distant from everyone else."

Now she *was* scared. How did he know about the loneliness, about the distance, about the fear of getting close because close was too dangerous. "But what if I don't know the kind of things you want to know?"

"There's nothing to know, Kessa. In therapy there are no wrong answers and no right answers. There's only the way you feel."

This was a little better, but she was still worried. "But what if the feelings don't make sense? What if I don't even know what the problem is?"

"That's what you and I are going to find out together. It won't happen today, Kessa, and it won't happen next week. The important thing, even if we don't see your problem clearly today, is that we do see signs of it."

"What do you mean?"

"Well, feeling uncomfortable is a sign of a problem. So is not being able to eat." He saw the look of fear pass across her face. "And so is not being able to stop eating. How much do you weigh?"

"I don't know," she lied.

"Listen, if you don't want to tell me, say you don't want to tell me, but I wish you wouldn't lie to me about it. That doesn't mean that if you say you don't want to talk about it, I won't still try to find out. I told you I'm going to invade your privacy, as much as I can and as often as I can, because I think some of that privacy is allowing you to make yourself unhappy.

"I guess your weight is something you think about."

She was silent for a moment. "Sometimes."

Sherman kept on like that for another half hour. He began to ask about her family and her friends and what she thought of them. Sometimes she answered. Often she didn't. When she didn't, he just kept talking.

"Well Kessa," he said at the end of the hour, "what do you think? Do you want to come back? Do you think we should start meeting twice a week?"

She shrugged.

"It's your decision."

128

"I guess so." Her voice was very low, but not so low that Sherman could not hear it.

After Kessa left the office, Sherman took a fresh folder and a sheet of paper and sat down at the small desk in the corner of the room to make a few notes. "Dietrich, Francesca," he wrote at the top of the page, then found he couldn't go on. He was remembering the girl's arms all bony and covered with hair and the way her jeans hung from her belt as if there was nothing inside them. He was treating two anorexics, but he'd begun to work with them after they'd been hospitalized and released. At times he'd worried that their physical condition was slipping again, but neither had ever looked as bad as this girl. Or seemed as distant. He needed time, time to build the kind of relationship that would allow him to banish the obsessions that were killing her, but time was exactly what he did not have. The thought that she might die before he could begin to help her hit with sudden force. Holding people's heads together was one thing, holding their bodies together something else. Goddamn it, he thought, if I wanted life-and-death situations, I would have become a surgeon.

Sherman heard the bell and knew his next patient had arrived. He hadn't made a single note, hadn't run down for the coffee he'd been looking forward to, hadn't even called his wife to say he'd be a little late this evening.

Before he left the office that night, he made the few notes he had never gotten to that afternoon.

Dietrich, Kessa (Francesca)—Ref'd Dr. E. Gordon. Diagnosis—A. N. *Severe*. Emaciated, withdrawn, mistrustful: has had previous unsatisfactory exp. in therapy. Lives w/both parents; has older sister (19) in Calif., older brother last year Harvard. Requests and demands are passive.

12

On Thursday morning Kessa arrived at Sherman's office carrying a container of coffee from the shop downstairs. She sat in the same chair as last time and removed the long-sleeved cotton shirt she had worn in anticipation of the air-conditioner. The day was cool for July, and Sherman had turned it off. When he saw her arms again, he almost wished he hadn't.

Kessa busied herself opening the container of coffee and placing it on a napkin on the table next to her. He noticed the way she aligned it with the edge of the table and placed the plastic stirrer carefully across the cardboard cover. It reminded him of a nurse laying out the instruments for surgery.

"Would you like some sugar?" he asked.

"No, thanks," she said quickly. "I had them put sugar in it downstairs."

"Kessa, when you ask for sugar downstairs, they give you a couple of little packages."

She began to cry. "You're just like all the rest of them" came through the muffled sobs.

"I'm sorry. I guess your thinness makes me a little anxious about your survival."

"Then why didn't you say that instead of all that business about sugar in my coffee? You were just trying to trap me."

"I wasn't trying to trap you, Kessa, and next time I'll tell you straight out without mentioning sugar. I guess we both need some practice getting used to each other."

"I don't want to talk about my weight. That's all anybody ever talks to me about anymore, and I just don't want to."

"I tell you what. Let's take each hour as it comes. I won't promise you not to talk about your weight, because eventually we're going to have to, but for today there are plenty of other things we can talk about. There is one thing I have to say about your weight though, Kessa. If you could gain a pound or two, it would help. Let me explain why before you get angry. I'd like to keep meeting with you like this, but if you keep losing weight, you're going to have to be hospitalized. You know that as well as I do. So if you could just gain a pound or two, we could keep you out of the hospital and go on with our meetings."

In response Kessa shed a pound and a half before her next appointment. During that hour Sherman asked her if she had been able to gain any weight.

"I guess I just haven't been very hungry," she lied, and changed the subject.

Despite her unwillingness to talk about food or her weight, the hour was far from unsuccessful. Sherman had the feeling she was already beginning to trust him. Before he went on to his next appointment, he scrawled a few notes in her file.

Listens attentively. Still has difficulty initiating talk. Is making eye contact more frequently. Comes on time. Doesn't watch clock. Beginning to ask for emotional contact though still masked with indifference. Tension in face.

Kessa too had felt the beginning of a bond. It terrified her. On the following Tuesday she stood in front of the building where his office was and stared at it. There was something menacing about the massive gray structure. *I'll walk around the block once,* she thought, *without stepping on a single crack. Then I'll be able to go in.* She circled the block twice without stepping on a single crack but still could not force herself to approach the heavy grilled door. *Maybe I'll get some coffee to take up with me.* She walked the few steps to Madison Avenue and entered the coffee shop on the corner. Quickly she counted the seats at the counter. Eleven. An uneven number. How could she possibly divide it? She counted five from the end. The next stool was empty. She sat down and counted five seats on each side of her.

Over the mirror behind the counter were signs suggesting various sandwiches. Her mental calculator began to function. Ham and cheese, five hundred seventy calories. Hamburger, three-fifty. Cheeseburger, five-forty. Grilled cheese, four-fifty. Grilled cheese with bacon, five-fifty. Kessa felt her stomach turn over as if it were a dog doing tricks in hope of being rewarded with a treat.

"What'll it be, honey?" The woman behind the counter was short and very round. Her large breasts and protruding stomach pulled against the thin pink nylon of her uniform. Kessa felt a wave of terror more acute than the one she'd experienced in front of Sherman's building.

"Nothing," she muttered, sliding from the stool and leaving the coffee shop at a run.

For the first five minutes Sandy welcomed Kessa's tardiness. He'd been running late all day, and the extra few minutes would give him a chance to return a few calls. By quarter after the hour, he'd begun to worry. By twenty-five after, he knew she wasn't coming, but he decided to wait till the end of the day to call. By that time Kessa might have telephoned herself.

At ten of seven when his last patient had left, he dialed the Dietrichs' number. "Mrs. Dietrich, this is Sandy Sherman. Your daughter didn't show up for her appointment today, and I was wondering if she's all right."

Grace was too tired of the problem to get angry. Her only feeling was "here we go again." "She left the house as if she was planning to keep her appointment, Dr. Sherman. And when she came home she seemed normal enough—if you can call not talking to anyone and locking herself in her room all afternoon normal."

"Could I speak to her now, please?" Sherman asked.

It took some time to get Kessa to the phone. She was sorry she hadn't kept the appointment that afternoon, but she was still afraid to talk to Sherman.

"I was worried about you when you didn't show up today, Kessa. I thought perhaps you were sick."

"Well, I just . . ." Her voice trailed off. She had no answer for him.

"You just what, Kessa?"

"Oh, I don't know. I guess I just didn't feel like going."

"I thought you said you wanted to go on
134

meeting with me." She did not answer. "If you do, I'll expect you to keep your appointments or to call me if you're too ill to keep one. But if you just don't show up this way, I can't treat you, Kessa. Is that clear? I'll expect to see you Thursday at the usual time. If you're not here, then I'll assume you've decided you don't want to go on seeing me and cross you off my schedule."

The words rang harshly in Kessa's ears. *Cross you off my schedule.* It sounded as if he were annihilating her.

Harold arrived home while his daughter was still on the phone. "What's all that about?" he asked Grace in an undertone.

"Sherman, the psychologist. Francesca didn't keep her appointment today."

"Goddamn it," he muttered.

"At least this one called right away," Grace pointed out, but Harold was not to be calmed.

"I thought you said you liked this one," he thundered when Kessa had hung up.

"He's all right, I guess."

"Then why the hell didn't you keep your appointment?"

"I don't know."

"You don't know! I don't understand you, Francesca. Don't you want to get better? Do you want to go on this way until you kill yourself?"

Now that her father's shouting had replaced Sherman's calm, firm voice, Kessa felt herself in control again. Without answering her father's accusations, she turned and left the room.

13

Kessa kept her next appointment, but it was too late. She had lost another pound. Evelyn Gordon called the following day.

"I'm afraid we're going to have to hospitalize Francesca Dietrich. She's down to seventy-two, and her blood pressure's so low I'm afraid she'll go into shock any minute. It's simply too dangerous to let her walk around like this."

For the hundredth time Sherman pictured the girl collapsing in his office. He had no medical training. He'd have no idea what to do. Kessa would die, and he'd be responsible. He had never had a patient close to death, and the idea alarmed him, just as the knowledge that he had failed her distressed him.

"I'm going to put her in Northeast," Evelyn Gordon continued. "There's an internist I work with there, Bernie Donaldson."

"I guess it had to happen." Try to sound rational, Sherman told himself, but he felt as if the sword that had been hanging over his head for the last two weeks had finally fallen.

"Don't sound so glum. I'm not putting her in psychiatric, so you're still on the case. And she was pretty far along when you got her. No one expects miracles."

Except maybe yourself, his wife would have told him.

"She is in the waiting room with her mother now. Donaldson is trying to get her a bed. He thinks they'll be able to admit her tomorrow morning. I told him you were on the case, but you'd better give him a call sometime tomorrow. Decide when you'll see her, things like that."

"I'll get in touch with him tomorrow."

Evelyn Gordon read the hesitancy in Sherman's voice. She would not have made a bad psychiatrist herself. "Don't let the hospital or the staff put you off. They may be a little reluctant to work with you at first, but just keep in mind that you're there for a reason, and when they see that, they'll come round. Who knows—they might even turn out to be cooperative." She laughed at her own optimism. "From my mouth to God's ear. Well, just keep at it and you're bound to get some coordinated care for the girl."

"I'll try."

"And one more thing, Sandy. She's pretty angry with me right now. I don't know whether she's going to hold you responsible too, but I thought I'd warn you."

"Well, you know what they say. Forewarned is forearmed." But there was no humor in his voice, and at ten of the next hour when the phone rang, he was not in the least prepared. At first he didn't recognize her voice through the sobs.

"I won't go to the hospital. Please don't make me go to the hospital."

"Kessa, I understand the idea is scary for you, but you're not being put in the hospital as a punishment. You're being put there to protect you, to make sure you won't die."

"But I don't want to go in. It sounds so final."

"It isn't final in the least. You'll be in the hospital until your physical condition permits you to leave. That doesn't mean I'm telling you to gain weight, Kessa." He wasn't going to make the same mistake twice. "You may hear that at home, but for the moment at least, you won't hear that again from me. I think if you could gain weight you would. But since you can't right now, the safest place for you is the hospital. But it isn't final and it isn't a punishment."

The only sound on the other end of the connection was her quiet, desperate sobbing.

"I'll go on seeing you while you're in the hospital—though you may not want to see me. But if you're willing to go on meeting, I'd like to."

Something in his voice, maybe simply the absence of any threat, set her off again, and she began to cry harder. "Please," she sobbed, "please, I'm begging you. Don't put me in the hospital."

He went through the same reasoning again, and by the time they had hung up she had stopped crying, though Sherman felt fairly sure she would start again at any moment. And he knew too that he would not shake off this call so easily. "Please, I'm begging you." The words continued to echo in his head even after he'd left his office—the words that seemed to accuse him of betrayal.

Sandy rarely had trouble sleeping, but that night he had to watch the late movie, read for an hour, fix himself a drink, then read for another hour before he could relax. Finally, close to four, he fell into a troubled, dreamful sleep. He was in a great barn and from the high, vaulted ceiling hung huge fishnets. When he looked up he saw they were filled not with fish but with dozens of naked corpses of emaciated girls. There was a good deal of activity at the far end of the barn, and he walked toward it. He saw the complicated mechanism. The girls were first hanged; then their bodies were flipped by means of a hinged beam into the nets. A man told him it was his job to place the rope around the girls' necks. Sherman protested, but his pleas fell on deaf ears. "Like it or not, buster, that's your job."

For the next several weeks, each time he saw Kessa, Sandy Sherman went home and dreamed the same dream.

14

After her parents had left the hospital, the nurse showed Kessa around the room, pointing out her narrow closet and two drawers, the bathroom, the controls for the television, the meal menu that had been left on her table. Kessa remembered a trip she'd taken with her parents to Montreal last fall. The nurse reminded her of the bellboy in the hotel. She seemed to think she was welcoming Kessa to some grand hotel. The more cheerful the nurse became, the more Kessa sulked. She'd done the same thing on the way to the hospital. The more her parents had tried to force conversation, the deeper Kessa had withdrawn into sullen silence. She'd show them. They might put her in the hospital, but she'd make them pay for it.

The nurse left, and Kessa sat on the end of her bed and looked around. There was another bed in the room, and the table next to it was cluttered with magazines, a comb, lipsticks, and a variety of perfectly familiar-looking objects. On the windowsill next to the other bed were a few stuffed animals. She obviously had a roommate, and from the looks of her things, she wasn't too sick either.

Kessa got up and walked to the unit below the

windows. She wanted to turn down the air-conditioner but couldn't figure out how it worked. *It's so damn cold*, she thought. *Anorexics are always cold*. It was the first time she'd thought of herself as an anorexic. The hospital was getting to her. She was beginning to believe she was sick after all.

"Hi, I'm Dr. Jarvis." A dark-haired man in white came striding into the room. Like the nurse who had just left, he seemed determinedly cheerful. "And you're Francesca Dietrich, right? Well, let's have a look at you."

"Where's Dr. Gordon?" It had been bad enough when Dr. Gordon told her she had to go into the hospital, but Kessa hadn't counted on a whole new contingent of strange doctors pushing and probing and telling her to eat.

"Who's Dr. Gordon?" Dr. Jarvis asked, running his fingers along the ridge girdling her rib cage, checking for distended liver, then spleen.

"My pediatrician." As soon as the words were out, Kessa cursed herself. Why hadn't she simply said doctor? She had sounded like a baby, and now they'd treat her like one and she'd have no control over herself at all.

"Well, while you're here you'll be in my care—I'm the chief resident—and 'here,' incidentally, is adolescent medicine. Dr. Donaldson will also see you, and so will Dr. Sherman, I understand." Jarvis saw no harm in giving the psychologist the honorary title. Perhaps it would help him establish some authority with this sullen, difficult girl.

"I don't call him doctor," she sulked.

"Well, whatever you call him, the three of us will be in charge of you." He completed the examination. "You seem to be in generally good health."

"Then why am I here?"

Jarvis wanted to tell her, "because you're a willful, impossible child," but if he did not have much faith in psychology, he had learned the advantages of tact. "To see that you stay that way."

"Do you put everyone in good health in the hospital to see they stay that way?" she taunted.

"Only those who don't seem to have the sense to stay that way on their own. So long, Francesca. I'll see you tomorrow."

Kessa stuck out her tongue at the empty doorway after Dr. Jarvis had left. Then she got up and took the chart from the end of the bed where he'd hung it. "Bilirubin elevated further. Possible non-specific hepatitis—monitor. Bradycardia. Pulse remains at 49. Blood pressure 80/50. Temp. 96.5." And at the bottom were scrawled the words "depressive—hostile." They were written larger than the rest of the report, almost as if Dr. Jarvis had been angry himself when he'd written them. But he hadn't seemed angry, Kessa thought. He hadn't seemed anything but totally unconcerned. He didn't give a damn about her. Nobody in this lousy place gave a damn about her.

Kessa picked up the phone and dialed her own number. Her mother would get her out. She'd find a way to make her mother get her out.

In the car driving away from Northeast Hospital neither Grace nor Harold spoke. The silence was welcome after the forced conversation of the ride with Francesca, but it was not comfortable. Each felt enormous relief—and was a little ashamed of the feeling. They were thinking too of the doctors' rules. No visits for the first month. Grace had lodged a lame protest, then backed down almost gratefully when told it was a hard and fast law in treating anorexics.

Harold spoke first. "At least she'll be safe there."

"That's what I keep telling myself," Grace answered. "It's the best place for her at this point."

They had come to a stoplight and each sat in silence, lost in solitary thought.

"Then why do I feel so goddamn guilty?" Harold burst out, and struck the steering wheel with his hand. "I'll tell you why. Because I'm glad she's there. Because I'm glad I don't have to look at her or worry about her or argue with her for a while."

"So am I," Grace said quietly.

But Hal was too overcome by his own guilt to hear her. "Sometimes I wish she was someone else's kid. Sometimes I wish we'd never had her. Isn't that a lousy thing to say, that I wish we'd never had our own kid?" His voice was choked by stifled sobs. It was something Grace had never heard.

"If you didn't care, Hal, you wouldn't be so upset." A horn sounded impatiently behind them. "Come on, we're making a traffic jam. Why don't we go somewhere for lunch, a nice lunch? I think we could both use one."

"When was the last time we had lunch alone like this?" Hal asked when they were seated in the restaurant and he had ordered a martini for each of them. It was as if Kessa's hospitalization had given them lives of their own again.

"I can't remember."

"Well, we ought to do it more often."

Grace agreed, though they both knew the chances of their doing it more often were slim. Still, Grace thought, even wanting to is a good sign.

144

"I guess that's one of the troubles with having a family," Hal continued. "It's always a family, never just the two of you anymore. Have you ever regretted having the kids, Grace? Have you ever been sorry?"

"Oh, there were moments when I was sorry, especially when they were small. There were times when I spent my days talking to three-year-olds, cleaning up spilled apple juice, screaming at Susanna not to hit her brother and Gregg not tease his sister. I'd have given anything to have a button I could push to make them disappear. But even then, it was only the button I wanted so I could push it again in a couple of hours and make them reappear. I never wished they didn't exist."

"Well, you know, I'm tired of being in the middle. I'm tired of taking care of the kids. I mean, we take care of everybody else, but no one seems to have time for us."

"Except us."

"You're right. That's what we started with, and that's what we're going to be left with. Well, I'll drink to it, Grace." He raised his glass toward her. "To you and me. You know, I kind of like that idea."

"So do I, Hal. So do I." And for the first time in weeks Francesca, even the absent Francesca, did not intrude.

When they walked into the apartment, the telephone was ringing. Grace heard the sound with a sinking stomach. It could have been Harold's office, it could have been anyone, but she knew it was Francesca.

"Well, you certainly took long enough getting home." Kessa's voice was an accusation, and within seconds Grace had tried herself for her pleasant lunch and found herself guilty.

"How are you, Francesca? How's the hospital?"

"It stinks. The doctors are mean and I'm bored stiff. I can't stand it here."

"I'm afraid you're going to have to stand it there until you're better." The words were firm, but Grace's voice was not—and Kessa heard the voice.

"Nasty doctors and bitchy nurses and lousy food"—the last was inspired, Kessa thought, since she hadn't been served a meal yet—"aren't going to make me better. I can't see why you'd put someone into the hospital to gain weight. Hospital food stinks. Everyone knows that."

Kessa had not missed her mark. Grace was aware there were many procedures the hospital could perform to keep her daughter alive—Dr. Gordon had listed them in grueling detail—but preparing appetizing food, Grace knew from experience, was not one of them.

"If there's some special treat you'd like, Francesca, just tell me and I'll try to arrange for it."

Kessa ignored the offer. "It's all disgusting."

"What's all disgusting?" Grace looked at her watch. Four o'clock. It was too early for dinner, even a hospital dinner, and Francesca had arrived after the institutional lunch hour of eleven-thirty. Suddenly Grace was angry. "Just what have they served you so far today that's so impossible to eat?"

"They brought in some milk and cookies this afternoon. They were awful."

"Did you taste the cookies?"

"I couldn't even stand to look at them."

"I am not taking you out of the hospital, Francesca, and that's final."

"But everyone is so mean." She thought of Dr. Jarvis's cold impersonality. "Nobody around here cares if I live or die."

146

Now the anger began to turn to worry as she thought of her frail daughter alone in that vast, anonymous hospital. "Listen, Francesca, I'll call Sandy Sherman in the morning to make sure everything is all right."

"You don't care about me either. You're just as bad as everyone else in this lousy place." Kessa slammed down the phone and buried her face in the pillow. She had been alone all afternoon, but someone might walk in at any minute, and she wasn't going to give anyone in this place the satisfaction of seeing her cry.

"What was that?" Harold asked when Grace had replaced the receiver.

"That was Francesca. She wants to come home. The place is terrible, the food is terrible . . ." Grace let her voice trail off. "And I feel terrible," she said finally.

The telephone started to ring again, but Harold got to it before his wife. He looked at her sitting abject and exhausted on the chair next to the phone. It was as if their lunch had never happened.

Harold's conversation with his daughter was briefer than Grace's. Francesca would have to stay in the hospital until she got better, he told her in what he himself would refer to as no uncertain terms. He replaced the receiver, stared at it for a moment, took it from its cradle, and placed it on the table.

"Hal, you can't."

"I can and I am going to. She's in the hospital, Grace. We put her there because it's the safest place for her. We can't do anything for her tonight. And remember what we said at lunch. It's you and I, Grace. We've got to take care of each other too. We had a nice lunch, and now I'd like to have a nice dinner and a nice evening without Francesca's threats and complaints." He walked to where she sat and put his arms around her. "I'd like to have a nice evening alone with you, Grace. Is that so much to ask?"

Grace did not answer him, but she held on to Harold as she had not for years, and after a while they both ceased to hear the buzzing sound of the phone that had been left off the hook.

Kessa had stopped crying by the time the girl who belonged to the next bed returned. They wheeled her in and moved her from the stretcher to her own bed, being careful not to jostle the leg encased in a large, awkward cast bent at the knee. After the nurse and orderlies left, the two girls eyed each other curiously. The other girl spoke first. She was black, and the slender high-cheekboned face contrasted sharply with the slightly overweight body.

"I figured I'd be getting a new roommate today. The girl who had your bed went home yesterday. She was white too." It was less a statement of hostility than one of fact. "My name's Lila. What's yours?"

"Kessa," she answered without debating the point. She almost never introduced herself as Francesca anymore.

"What you here for?"

"Nothing . . . really."

Lila looked at her with disbelief but decided that whatever her new roommate suffered from, it might be too painful to talk about with a stranger. "They operated on my leg. I had a clubfoot. They had to break the bones and everything."

Kessa said nothing, and Lila decided to try a nonmedical tack. "You live around here?"

148

"In Manhattan. Central Park West."

"I got a friend who lives a couple of blocks from there." Lila did not offer the friend's name, and Kessa did not ask it. Both knew they would be unlikely to move in the same world, beyond the small one of Northeast Hospital.

An elderly woman came in with two trays. She was not unkind, but she gave the appearance of brooking no nonsense. Lila picked up the metal cover and looked at the plate before her. "Ugh. Salisbury steak again. You know, before I came to this place, I didn't know what Salisbury steak was— or maybe I knew what it was, but I sure as hell didn't call it by such a fancy name. Well, it ain't much, but at least it ain't their worst." Lila noticed that Kessa had stopped talking to her as soon as the trays arrived. I got the snotty one this time, she thought, switching on the television. Then she turned back to the Salisbury steak.

Kessa did not even bother to lift the metal cover. It didn't matter what was under it. The hospital had merely intensified her fear of food, and since there was no one there to tell her to eat, she didn't have to make any pretense. When the woman came to take the trays away, Kessa's was still untouched.

The woman looked from the tray to Kessa. "I thought you was one of those."

"One of those what?"

"The skinnies. There's only one other on the floor now, but we get them in and out pretty regular. You look pretty far along too. I bet in a couple of days they'll start putting those needles in you." She eyed the tray. "At least they will if you don't start eating." The woman looked the thin figure in the

149

pajamas and robe up and down carefully. "You're probably going to start having trouble walking soon, too."

"How do you know so much? You're not a doctor," Kessa shot back, surprised at her own bravery. "You're not even a real nurse."

"No, but I been on this floor long enough to see a couple of you, and you're all the same."

Kessa wanted to scream that she wasn't the same as anyone, but the woman's authority terrified her. Would she have trouble walking soon? Was she just like them?

"Well, at least you don't pull any of the disgusting stuff . . . yet."

"Disgusting stuff?"

"Yeah. Some of them hide food in their beds. Some of them throw up in the bathroom. But it looked to me like you just don't eat." The woman picked up the tray and left the room, radiating disapproval.

"So that's what's wrong with you," Lila said.

"No, it isn't. She made a mistake."

"Well, is sure looks like it is. You're just as thin as all the skinnies, and you didn't eat nothin'. So I guess that makes you a skinny."

"I wish you wouldn't call me that."

"Why not? I'm black and I call myself black. You're a skinny and I'm goin' to call you one. You don't like it, then stop actin' funny like one and I'll stop callin' you one."

15

On her way to the kitchen to make coffee the next morning, Grace put the receiver back on the hook. The phone rang immediately.

"You took the phone off the hook," Kessa accused.

It was too early. Grace was too defenseless. The guilt washed over her. "I'm sorry, Francesca, but I was not going to spend the entire night arguing with you. Did you have a good night?"

"How could I in this place. I couldn't sleep with all the noise," she lied. Kessa had been so exhausted from the tension and lack of food that she had slept long, if not deeply. "And dinner was so awful I couldn't touch it."

"How did you know it was awful if you didn't taste it?" But the counterattack did nothing to reassure Grace.

"Have you called Sandy Sherman?"

"Francesca, it's seven o'clock in the morning. I can't call him yet."

"Are you going to call him and tell him to get me out of here?"

"I'm going to call him to make sure you're being cared for."

"Well, I'm not being cared for. I had a stomach-ache last night, and nobody gave a damn. I stood around the nurses' station forever, and nobody did anything."

Once again Grace's own experience flooded back over her. She remembered when her father had been in the hospital after his heart attack. Her mother had insisted on private nurses for him. "It isn't their fault," Emily had conceded. "The nurses are overworked. Still, I won't have your father's needs being overlooked. He'll have to have private care."

Were Francesca's needs being overlooked now? Were the nurses too busy to pay attention to a stomachache?

"I'll call Sandy Sherman at eight, Francesca, and I'll call you right back after I speak to him."

"Fat lot of good that's going to do. I don't want you to call back. I want you to come and get me out of here."

Harold walked into the kitchen dressed for the office. He could tell from his wife's face who was on the other end of the line.

"I'll call you after I speak to Sandy Sherman, Francesca. Good-bye."

"I see you put the phone back on the hook," Hal said.

"We can't very well wash our hands of her completely."

"No, I guess we can't," he said, and opened the *Times* to the business section.

Driving to his office that morning, Sandy Sherman was thinking more of Kessa's hospitalization than he was of Kessa. It was the first time he had treated a patient in hospital, and now the original feeling of failure at having to admit the girl was accompanied by fear. He was an outsider to that world. It was a closed club, and he did not belong. How were they going to treat him? And how successful was he going to be in treating her if he was continually worrying about his own professional problems? When he'd called to inquire whether she'd been admitted yesterday, he'd identified himself as Dr. Sherman, and the woman in the admissions office had mistaken the Ph.D for an M.D. and treated him with the customary deference. But on the floor itself things would be different. Sandy remembered the stories and warnings psychologists traded. "Stay out of hospitals. You'll be low man on the totem pole." "To an M.D. a psychologist is less than nothing." "They'll fight you at every turn."

By the time Sherman arrived at his office, he had worked himself into something between rage and panic. It wasn't only pride, he told himself. It was a question of giving Kessa the best possible care, and he couldn't do that without the staff's cooperation.

He decided to begin by following Evelyn Gordon's advice and dialed Dr. Donaldson's number. Donaldson cut through his introduction. He'd been expecting him.

"Jarvis—that's the chief resident—saw her yesterday. He said she's okay except for the liver. Bilirubin elevated. There's a slow heartbeat and low body temperature too, but we've come to accept that as normal for emaciated anorexics. It's as if they're in hibernation."

The medical terms were a good omen, Sandy thought. He's treating me like an equal. Goddamn it, I am an equal. I've got to watch it or that hospital mentality is going to get to me.

"That," Donaldson continued, "and she's hostile as hell."

"I was afraid of that. I'd like to see her this afternoon."

"Whenever you say."

Whenever *he* said. Well, at least he hadn't been condescended to.

Sandy Sherman hung up the telephone feeling a lot better about himself—but considerably worse about Kessa. "Hostile as hell," Donaldson had said. He wondered how much of that hostility was going to spill over on him and destroy the little trust he'd begun to establish. Before he could begin to think about it, the phone rang.

"Dr. Sherman, this is Grace Dietrich, Francesca's mother. I've just spoken with her. She's terribly upset. She called last night and"—Grace had begun to say that she probably would have kept calling all night if they hadn't taken the phone off the hook, but she still felt too guilty to admit it—"and she called again this morning and said she simply can't stay there."

"Why can't she stay there, Mrs. Dietrich?"

The calmness of his voice and the simplicity of the question threw her off balance. What could she say? That the doctors were mean and the nurses bitchy? "She complained about the food."

"Isn't that one of the reasons Kessa's in the hospital? Because she's been complaining about the food, because she's been refusing to eat?"

"Kessa. You call her Kessa?"

"That's the way she introduced herself. I assumed it was a nickname."

"If it is, I've never heard it before. Her friends call her—or rather her friends used to call her—Francesca. She even went through a stage when she insisted on being called her full name, Francesca Louise. I thought it was ridiculous, but she said if I named her Francesca Louise I ought to be willing to call her Francesca Louise. Even when she was little, her logic could do me in."

"Or what appears to be her logic."

"What do you mean?"

"I'm sure Kessa's presenting what seems like logical arguments to you, Mrs. Dietrich. For example, if you want her to gain weight, why did you put her in a hospital, where food is notoriously bad? But in fact Kessa is not only not logical now, she isn't even competent. If she was, she wouldn't be lying in a hospital bed nearly dead of starvation. Try to remember that next time Kessa begins to manipulate you."

"Manipulate me?"

"I have a feeling she does it fairly often. Kessa's involved in a struggle with herself, and I think she's extended it to the rest of the family. Most anorexics do this, you know. Your daughter's engaged in a power struggle with you and your husband, Mrs. Dietrich. I'm not suggesting her problem is as simple as that, but I am suggesting her need to manipulate you is part of the problem, a part we're all going to have to work on."

Grace was silent for a moment thinking about Sherman's words. Which of Francesca's words were true and which were lies to get her mother to do as she wanted? She remembered the story about the stomachache. "She complained that she had a stomachache last night and no one paid any attention. She said she went to the nurses' station and no one had time for her."

"Did Kessa say what she did when she got to the nurses' station, Mrs. Dietrich? Did she ask for

155

help or did she simply stand around looking sullen?" Grace did not answer. Sherman's words seemed to make sense, but she wasn't sure she could be that hardhearted. "I don't mean to sound harsh, Mrs. Dietrich, but we have to be careful. We can't let Kessa continue to manipulate, and we have to be especially wary of letting her pit you against me or against any of the doctors. I suspect that's one of the things that keep girls like Kessa from getting well. And we can't allow her to keep herself from getting well."

"I think I'm going to need some help with this myself, Dr. Sherman. Perhaps my husband and I could meet with you?"

"I was thinking of that. I think a family meeting will be helpful, but I want to check with Kessa first. I don't say I'll let her veto it, but she'll probably have to be convinced of the idea."

Grace's second conversation with her daughter that morning was, despite Sherman's advice and calming effect, no more satisfactory than the first. Kessa slammed the phone down in a rage, sure that her mother and Sandy were now in league against her. And she had been certain he was on her side—or at least could be recruited to her side to be used against her parents.

Furious at them both, Kessa left her room to explore the floor. She had stayed in her room most of the day before, and the single time she had ventured out into the hall, she had been oblivious to everything around her. It had seemed more important at the time to concentrate on getting out. Now that they were going to keep her here, she might as well find out something about the setup.

There were several teenagers wandering about the hall. Most wore robes, but a few were dressed normally. Kessa began to wonder what each of them was here for. Sometimes the problem was made obvious by a pair of crutches or bandage or wheelchair, but often, especially when they were dressed normally, there seemed to be no particular reason for their presence here. Some of them were laughing and talking as if they were in school, and the sound of rock music blared from several rooms.

Kessa noticed one girl wearing jeans and a sweater walking rapidly up and down the corridor. Actually she had noticed the girl immediately but had tried not to look at her. The girl was horribly thin, and her clothes hung on her as they would on a hanger. As the girl passed her, she looked curiously at Kessa, but Kessa kept her eyes fixed straight ahead. The girl was obviously what the nurse's aide called a skinny, and Kessa couldn't stand the sight of skinnies.

Escape, however, was not as easy as Kessa thought. When she returned to her room a few minutes later, the girl followed.

"Hi, I'm Myrna." The girl came striding into the room as if she owned it. "You're an anorexic, aren't you?" When Kessa said nothing, she continued. "Yeah, I knew you were. I can always spot them. We're the only two here now. There was another one last week, but she went home. In the last hospital I was in, there were four of us at one time."

"The last hospital?" Kessa asked almost against her will.

"Yeah, I've only been here two weeks, but I was in the other one for seven months. I got out of there . . ."

"How'd you get out?"

"You make a deal with them. Find out how

much weight they want you to gain and gain it. Then as soon as you get home you can take it off again."

"Is that why they put you back in here?"

"No, I'm here for observation. They're trying to find a drug to stop me from bingeing."

"Bingeing?"

"Boy, you've got a lot to learn," Myrna said, clearly eager to instruct this novice in the more sophisticated methods of their madness. "Bingeing is going all out. You know, when you hit the fridge and eat your way straight through it in one sitting. I do it all the time. Before they put me in I was doing it every day. I'm probably the world's best binger."

"Then how come you're not fat?" Kessa was skeptical of Myrna's story.

"Like I said, you've got a lot to learn. Haven't you ever heard of vomiting?"

Kessa recoiled from the word and the vivid picture it produced. Then the picture of this tall, skinny girl vomiting turned into an image of Kessa herself leaning over the toilet in her own bathroom. "How disgusting."

"Well, it isn't much fun—I'll give you that— but at least it keeps me from gaining weight."

"It seems it would be easier just not to binge."

"Easy to say. Anyway now they're looking for some drug to stop me. They think there's something wrong with my head that makes me binge, something physical. I've been to lots of shrinks, and they couldn't do anything at all, so now they think they'll find a drug to make whatever's wrong right."

"How long are they going to keep you here?" Kessa returned to her own immediate problem.

Myrna shrugged. "Who knows?"

"Don't you care?"

"Not much. Sometimes I think maybe I'd like to go home, but then my family shows up and I don't want to after all. And everytime I do go home it's awful. Besides, I'm becoming a pro."

"A pro?"

"Yeah. I know how everything works now and how to get around it. They're pretty strict with us, stricter than if you broke your leg or something like that, but you'll find out soon enough. They watch every mouthful you eat and where what you don't eat goes. And they keep track of your weight like goddamn hawks, but it's all a lot of bullshit, and if you really want to, you can get around it all."

"I don't want to get around it, I just want to get out."

Myrna was beginning to be bored by this naive kid. "Then make a deal and gain as much as they want you to." Myrna shrugged and left the room for another bout of hallway hiking. She had figured out exactly how many times she had to travel the floor to use up a single calorie.

Kessa turned to Lila, who had been reading a magazine throughout her exchange with Myrna.

"Well, she's a skinny all right," Kessa said.

"She's crazy."

"I guess you think I'm crazy too."

"Not as crazy as her." Lila was thoughtful for a moment. "You know, before I came here I never heard of whatever that thing you have is. I mean, who'd think anybody could be crazy enough to starve themselves to death? The thing is I only found out about this sickness when I started hangin' out with you white girls. I don't think any black

159

people ever had anything like it. I guess what you got is a white disease the way sickle-cell is a black one."

"But why is it a white disease?" It seemed to Kessa that if she knew something about it, she might learn something about herself.

Lila looked at her hard. Her eyes were skeptical and not especially kind. "I don't know, but I bet it's 'cause white people ain't generally hungry."

"I'm hungry all the time."

"Not hungry 'cause you're dietin', hungry 'cause you ain't got enough food. Like blacks. You always had enough food, so you can make a game out of it. Maybe when blacks have enough they'll start makin' a game out of it too."

"But it isn't a game. You don't understand. It's real, more real than anything else. I'm scared to death of eating too much. After I eat I'm terrified, and I don't even know why."

Lila was still skeptical. "After I eat I'm sorry cause I broke my diet, but I just go on breakin' it and tellin' myself I won't."

"I wish I could make a joke out of it."

"Well, maybe it ain't no joke to you, but I still say it's a game."

Kessa wondered if anyone, including herself, could understand the panic she felt. Even the other skinny, Myrna, hadn't seemed to feel the same terror. Kessa was drowning in a sea of fear, and no one could understand it. And if no one could understand it, no one could save her.

16

During Kessa's next two appointments with Sherman she was more silent and sullen than she had been at any time since their first meeting. She refused to answer his questions, would not even give him the satisfaction of raising her eyes to his as he sat in the small office they used for their meetings and told her again and again the things she must be feeling. Kessa was still amazed that he could know these things, but she was determined to punish him for letting them put her in the hospital.

Then a curious thing happened. On the day Kessa decided to relent—she'd grown tired of punishing the only person who seemed to understand her even a little—Sherman decided to change his approach. He knew from their talks that Kessa had a history of manipulating the doctors who had tried to treat her. They had all been eager to win her. He decided to play hard to get. Sherman knew he was taking a terrible chance. Now that he had access to her medical chart at every visit, he could see her condition sinking. He was becoming well versed in the various medical dangers that threatened her. From what he'd learned so far, Sandy knew he'd never treated anyone this close to death. Her condition necessitated drastic measures—and at the same time made him terrified of using them.

He came into Kessa's room to get her, but instead of helping her down the hall as he usually did—the nurse's aide had been right; Kessa could barely hold herself upright to walk—he hurried along ahead of her. The pain Kessa felt as the soles of her feet, stripped of all padding, hit the floor through her thin slippers was nothing compared to the fear of losing Sandy Sherman. After they had been sitting in the room and talking for a few minutes, he stood abruptly and looked at his watch.

"They told me they need this room at two, Kessa. We'll have to change offices." Once again he raced, and Kessa limped after him in desperate pursuit. Sandy never knew exactly what mechanism he had triggered, but Kessa began to talk to him again.

She did not, however, begin to gain weight. Even the pain that had become a constant reminder of her condition could not cut through the wall of fear that kept her from eating. Her body was wracked by aches and pains, the residue of a series of falls because she was too weak to walk, the by-product of uncushioned bones meeting hard chairs, hard floor, hard surfaces of every kind. And the cold. She was always cold now. Still the pounds dropped off. She had been in the hospital four days now and had lost two and a half pounds. Each time they had brought her a meal, she had let it sit untouched on the plate.

Kessa dropped off to sleep without realizing it. When she awakened, Dr. Donaldson was standing over her bed with the chart, the concrete indictment of her illness, in his hands. At least it wasn't Dr. Jarvis. Donaldson wasn't nearly as cold as Jarvis.

"Well, Kessa, you've lost another half a pound. I explained what would happen if you lost any more weight." There was no recrimination in his voice, only sorrow. "We'll have to start hyperalimentation."

It had happened finally. The tubes, the force-feeding, all the terrible things they had been warning her of for months were finally going to happen.

"Will it hurt?"

"There'll be some discomfort while the surgeon does the procedure."

The surgeon. Still another doctor to push and prod and torture her. Sandy Sherman was one thing. You couldn't really call him a doctor, although some of the nurses and other doctors did. And she had gotten used to Dr. Donaldson. But she still hated Dr. Jarvis, and now they were going to foist another one on her, and this one was going to cut into her.

"But I don't need surgery," she whimpered. "I just can't eat."

"I know, Kessa. That's why we're going to perform this procedure—to make sure you get enough nutrition to keep you alive."

Nutrition. The word hit her with sudden force. She forgot the fear of pain, the hatred for another doctor. She was threatened by a more terrible danger now. They were going to make her fat. They were going to stick a tube in her chest—Myrna had showed Kessa her own marks; they had done it to her three different times—and pour calories into her until she swelled and swelled into some huge fat-riddled animal. She'd swell and swell until she exploded, and then there'd be no more wonderfully bony body and no more Kessa. There'd be no more anything, and there was nothing she could do about it. They had taken her body from her control.

Dr. Donaldson went on talking, and the words came to her distantly through the fog of her own fear. " . . . local anesthetic. They'll insert a catheter —that's a tube—at this point." He touched her chest just below her collarbone, and his finger felt icy against her skin. "They'll tape the tube to your shoulder, and the bottle will be on a stand with wheels. You'll be walking around with it in no time. And in four or five days we'll have enough nutrition in you . . ."

His voice faded out, and she was thinking of Francesca Louise, the fantasy queen of Central Park West, the girl who could will her friends to be the people she chose, the world to be the way she wanted it. And then she was thinking of Kessa, the girl who was pure movement, free of ugly bodily needs, free of other people and other opinions, free of everything but the mad adulation of the throngs she danced before. But Kessa the prima ballerina gave way to Kessa the invalid trapped in a hospital bed, Kessa the helpless skeleton force-fed by powers beyond her control.

" . . . and you probably won't be able to eat or drink anything at first. That won't last long, maybe twenty-four hours, but for that period we'll put a sign over your bed that says NPO. That means nothing by mouth. But you won't be hungry, because all your nutritional needs will be met intravenously."

Won't be hungry. If only he knew. It was bad enough when she chose not to eat, but if they kept her from eating she'd do nothing but think about food all day.

164

"Any questions, Kessa?"

She shook her head, unable to speak. It was taking all her strength to hold back the tears until he left. After he had gone she gave way to them.

Lila heard the sobs just as she had the doctor's words. "Hey, Kessa, don't cry. He said it don't hurt."

"But I'm scared. I'm just so scared."

"Listen, I know it's scary. When they wheeled me up for my foot I was scared shitless, but they knocked me out right away, and it was over before I knew anything."

"But they're not going to put me out, and it's probably going to hurt, and the worst of it is they're going to pump something into me to make me gain weight. They're going to make be fat."

Lila lost patience. "Maybe you are crazy. Just like crazy Myrna," she said, and switched on the television.

Sandy Sherman sat in his office staring blankly out the window. There wasn't much of a view to begin with, but this morning he didn't even notice the drab courtyard. He was thinking of Kessa and the phone conversation he'd just had with Bernie Donaldson.

"Our girl's lost another half pound," Bernie had begun. "Down to sixty-nine and a half. We've got to do something. It's either an IV or hyperalimentation, and I'm for hyperalimentation."

"Isn't that kind of drastic?"

"Her condition is drastic. Her bilirubin is elevated. BUN is indicating incipient renal dysfunction. Bradycardia is accompanied by cardiac arrhythmia. Renal dysfunction probably due to low

165

blood supply and an overwhelming concentration of toxins overworking the kidneys. Well, that's all three now. Heart, liver, and kidneys. There are a lot of advantages to hyperalimentation," Donaldson continued. "For one thing, we can keep her going much longer that way, and in this case I think that might be necessary. An IV, since it's only the diameter of a syringe, is just a temporary measure. With hyperalimentation, nutrition flows through a wide-bone tube, and we can keep her alive for months. And it'll give her TPN—total parenteral nutrition—in a form that can be metabolized. It means we can send everything she needs to stay alive straight into her bloodstream."

Sherman tried to remember the fragments of information he'd picked up about hyperalimentation. They didn't add up to much, but he did remember one thing. "Isn't there a good chance of infection? I mean, going straight into the jugular vein that way?"

"There's some, but we've been doing it for a couple of years at Northeast now, and I think we've got it down pat. Even with all the anorexics we've had up in adolescent medicine, there hasn't been any incidence of infection."

"Then you're definitely in favor of hyperalimentation rather than an IV?" Sherman was hedging. He couldn't drive the picture of the frail child he'd seen yesterday afternoon from his mind, and the idea of inserting a catheter directly into her jugular vein unnerved him.

"It's partly the shape she's in now," Donaldson continued. "I think she needs more than the meager nutrition we can drip in with a regular IV. But more than that, I'm worried about the future. I don't see how we're going to keep her alive without hyper-alimentation. If you want to know the truth, I don't know how we're going to keep her alive at all. I've treated a lot of these kids, and I've never seen one of them get well. I've seen them leave the hospital and come back and spend the rest of their lives on that merry-go-round, but in this case, I don't see how we can hope for even that little. She's one of the most recalcitrant I've ever seen. She just won't eat. That's why I'm in favor of hyperalimentation. I think you're going to have a hell of a job getting to her at all, and I'd like to have some margin for error."

"You mean for failure."

"Don't take it personally, Sandy. I've seen you with her. If anybody can get through, it's probably you. The thing is, I just don't think anyone can get through to these kids. We can manage them, but I just don't think we can cure them. But that's neither here nor there. If you're in agreement about the hyperalimentation, I'll set it up with the surgeon for tomorrow morning."

By the time Sandy Sherman got off the phone, he was too upset about Kessa and what he was letting happen to her to notice that not only had Donaldson not condescended to him, but he had called him to confer on the course of treatment for their patient. At any other time Sherman would have been euphoric. This morning he was merely grim, and that night the dream recurred with a new vividness. He wondered if he was becoming too involved with her.

Kessa too slept badly that night. At about two in the morning, she awoke with a start. She knew she had been dreaming, but she couldn't

167

remember the dream. The room was dark, and she couldn't tell if she had just fallen asleep or if it was almost morning. She was totally disoriented.

Then she remembered the tube they were going to put in her the next morning. How much weight would she gain? Where would it go? She ran her hands over her body as if to bid it good-bye. The hipbones rising from a shrunken stomach were razor-sharp. Would they be lost in a sea of fat? She counted her ribs, bone by bone. Where would they go? She squeezed one arm and then the other. Would they blow up like great puffed sleeves of flesh? She pressed against her stomach till the pain was excruciating. There was so little time before they put the tube in. If only she could lose a few more pounds.

The waking nightmare was too much for her. Kessa struggled to get out of bed, but it was no longer a simple maneuver. As she rolled over on her side she could feel the pain all along her body. It was as if the mattress were made of rock. She swung her legs down and jerked her body into a sitting position, but she had to cling to the edge of the bed to keep from toppling off. The room whirled around her, and she felt as if she were falling, falling, falling. Kessa sat that way, clutching the edge of the bed and trying to regain her balance, for several minutes. When the dizziness had passed, she decided she was ready to stand. She wasn't sure where she was going—to the nurses' station, to the bathroom, nowhere at all—but she knew she could not stay in bed thinking of the weight she was going to gain.

As her feet hit the ground, the pain echoed through her legs. The room began to whirl again, and then there was nothing at all.

Lila probably would not have been awakened by her roommate's fall if Kessa's frail body hadn't collided with the night table. As it was, Lila, groggy with sleep, heard the noise and switched on her bed light. She saw Kessa lying in a heap on the floor and rang for the nurse.

A nurse came, called another, got Kessa back into bed, and summoned the intern on duty. For the next half hour Lila lay awake listening to the sounds coming from behind the curtain they had pulled around Kessa. She could hear the girl crying and the nurses reassuring her and the doctor's voice tense and commanding above it all. "She's going into shock . . . on the verge of complete circulatory collapse . . . IVs in both wrists, glucose in the left, plasma in the right . . . I want a cardiac monitor . . . get me an oxygen mask . . . cover her up, she's got no body heat . . ."

And through it all Lila could hear Kessa's familiar plaint. "Am I going to gain weight? Is this going to make me fat?"

"What's her pressure now?" The doctor's voice cut through Kessa's sobbing.

"Back up to seventy-five over forty-five."

"Terrific." Lila recognized the anger in the doctor's voice. "Stay with her, Elaine, for the next hour at least. I don't want those IVs infiltrated. If they block, she'll go into shock and that'll be the end."

Finally the doctor left the room and the nurses pulled the curtain back. Lila could see the tubes running from the bottles suspended above the bed into both Kessa's arms. There was a nurse sitting beside the bed. "Is she okay?" Lila asked.

"She is now."

Lila could tell from the way she said it that she hadn't been for a while there. It seemed im-

169

possible that someone her own age could die, but she supposed from all the excitement and talk that Kessa had come close to it.

"You sure did shake the place up," Lila said to her roommate the next morning.

"I don't remember what happened."

"You fainted—or somethin' like that. I was asleep and I heard a big noise, and next thing I know there you are lyin' on the floor like a heap of old rags."

"Did you call the nurse?" Kessa asked.

"I would've got you up myself, but I ain't exactly up to it with this cast."

"Thanks for calling the nurse."

"I guess you must be in lousy shape. I mean, if you can't even stand up without faintin'."

Kessa said nothing.

Lila was impatient again. The girl was clearly loony. "So skinny you can't even stand up, and all you do is worry about gainin' weight. If that ain't playin' games, I don't know what is."

After Lila went back to sleep, Kessa lay watching the IV dripping into her arm. There was just enough light in the room to see the drops falling into the tiny reservoir below the full bottle and then into the transparent tube. Drip, drip, drip. Fat, fat, fat. The drops moved into her relentlessly, one after another, filling her up. There must be a way to stop it. Kessa tried to contract the muscles in her arm. Drip, drip, drip. She made the arm tighter. It felt as if it were on fire, but still the liquid continued. Drip, drip, drip.

She had lost. The thinner would be the winner, and she almost had been; but now they'd started this, and she could never be the winner with this.

Kessa thought of the models and of the pictures she had torn up. She imagined herself going through the wastebasket piecing each torn picture back together again. The liquid continued to run into her body, and now the tears ran down her face in silent, helpless despair.

She didn't know how much later it was—a half hour, an hour, two—when two nurses came and wheeled her into another room. Then Dr. Donaldson came in with a group of other doctors. "Kessa, this is Dr. Meyer. He's going to do this procedure I explained to you yesterday." Dr. Donaldson introduced the others, but Kessa could look only at the one called Meyer, the one who was going to stick the tube in her.

Meyer had greeted her gruffly and began to speak to the men clustered around her. As he talked he pushed and prodded at Kessa as if she were a demonstration doll. "The catheter will be inserted at this point"—his index finger jabbed just below her collarbone—"and should intercept the jugular vein roughly two inches above the heart. It will be monitored constantly to see that it does not infiltrate —drift through the wall of the vein and tear or clog it. It must be checked daily to see that antiseptic ointment is adequate and no infection develops at the incision, which remains open. Taping the line at several points prevents any movement at the opening or incision and prevents infection. The patient ..."

Kessa wanted to scream at him. *The patient! I'm the patient, me, Kessa, Francesca Louise, an individual,* but she lay there in silence listening to him drone on.

" ... will be able to sit, stand, and walk about, since the bottle will be placed on a stand with casters. After we have ascertained her pancreatic tolerance for glucose, we will gradually increase the contents of the hyperalimentation until total parenteral nutrition is arrived at. In most cases we can expect that to happen in four or five days. The procedure itself takes only about half an hour." As if the words had been a signal, Dr. Meyer turned from his colleagues to Kessa.

"Now, you'll have to lie perfectly straight and look up at the ceiling." One of the nurses helped her take off her robe and hospital gown, arranged her in the position Dr. Meyer had dictated, and pulled the sheet halfway up her chest. The nurse tucked that sheet into the mattress, then placed another diagonally across Kessa's chest and stomach.

"I'm going to give you several injections that will numb the area," Dr. Meyer said, leaning over her exposed left shoulder and breast. He was supposed to be talking to Kessa, but she had the feeling he was really speaking to the other doctors. "Now, keep looking at the ceiling and don't move your head."

Then they started. The first sting came high up in the center of her chest. Kessa fought to keep back the tears. A second stung lower, and a third felt as if it were sticking into her rib. The fourth, below her arm, was the worst of all. The last injection seemed to go on forever, and then she felt the pain surging up her back through her neck to the base of her skull. It was a river of pain flowing from her ribs to her head, and she clamped her mouth together to keep from screaming.

"Don't move your left arm," Dr. Meyer said. His hands were working rapidly over the table of instruments Kessa had seen them wheel in. They

172

were out of her view now, and she wondered what horror was coming next.

Out of the corner of her eye Kessa could see the nurses fidgeting with bottles and tubes on a stand similar to the one they'd hooked her up to last night. She was torn between wanting to watch and needing to shut the whole thing out of her consciousness.

She felt an itch on her left thigh and reached to scratch it. A knifelike pain shot through her left shoulder, and she cried out. It was the first sound she'd made since they'd begun.

"I'm afraid that shoulder will become a little stiffer before we're through." For the first time Dr. Meyer sounded almost apologetic. He began a second round of injections. They followed the pattern of the first, but there were six this time.

She realized Dr. Meyer was watching her face now. "Just trying to make sure we've got you numb enough." He said it as if it were a joke, but he was watching carefully for every indication of pain. "Now, just keep looking at the ceiling."

She began to feel a sticking feeling in her chest. No, not a sticking feeling, a drilling feeling. It felt as if he were drilling a hole in her chest.

He looked down at her face. "Are you feeling this?"

Instead of saying yes, she nodded, and a pain shot through her neck and shoulder.

"More novocaine," Dr. Meyer snapped. One of the nurses handed him something quickly. Kessa could tell from the motion of his hands that he was giving her more injections, but she could no longer feel them.

The day nurse was wiping the tears from Kessa's

face, but the faster she wiped, the faster they flowed. *I want my mommy, I want my mommy* raced again and again through Kessa's mind.

Dr. Meyer asked for another instrument, and the drilling turned into a dull, picking sensation. Then the picking sharpened, and it felt as if something were being inserted in her chest. Whatever it was went sliding, bumping, and poking its way inside her chest.

"Sutures," Dr. Meyer demanded. He was bending over her, and she could feel his breath on her face, but at least the pain had stopped.

"You're getting pretty good at this, Mel." Dr. Donaldson spoke for the first time since they had started this torture.

"I should be," Meyer said. "When I was a kid I could always get the coins through the sewer grates with gum and a string better than any kid on the block." All the men in white began to laugh, and Kessa wanted to scream until she had driven every one of them from the room. For what seemed like an eternity they had been pricking and drilling and cutting and sewing her body, and now they all laughed as if it had been a great joke. *Mommy,* she thought, *I want my mommy.*

One of the nurses began rubbing a cream around the area where the doctor had been working and then bandaged it. Dr. Meyer straightened and began to rub his lower back and rotate his neck. "Keep bringing in these starving kids at this rate, Bernie, and I'll be able to do it with my eyes closed." He turned to Kessa and stroked the top of her head. "Take my advice. Eat through your mouth. It's a lot easier.

"Now, your left arm is going to be stiff around

the shoulder for a while. When you've gained some strength, you'll be able to walk around with that thing."

As Dr. Meyer turned to leave, Kessa spoke for the first time. "How much weight will I gain?"

Meyer looked at her in disbelief. No matter how many of them he worked on, he could never understand them. "You'd better ask Dr. Donaldson about that. I'm just the plumber."

Kessa opened her eyes and saw Sandy Sherman standing over her bed. "Hi, how are you feeling?" he asked as if nothing had happened.

Trapped, she wanted to scream, but instead she said, "When can I go home?"

"When you're healthy enough."

"When's that?"

"It's hard to predict—and partly up to you."

"In other words, you won't tell me when I can go home."

"That sounds like an accusation, Kessa."

She turned her head away from him, but her eyes lighted on the bottle. "That thing. It's going to make me fat."

"It won't make you fat, Kessa, but it will return you to some semblance of health. You were a very sick girl. You almost died two nights ago."

"Oh, sure."

"Listen Kessa, I'm sorry to have to say this, but we have to get something straight. When it comes to yourself and your health, you're simply not a competent judge. And because you're not, Dr. Donaldson and I are taking over. We're responsible for you now. If you want something, you channel the request through us, because we're completely in

175

charge of you and we're going to do our best to keep you safe from yourself and any medical danger. Is that clear?"

"How much weight is this thing going to put on me?"

"That isn't to fatten you up, Kessa; it's to bring you out of medical danger. We'll keep you on it till you reach anywhere from seventy-two to seventy-five pounds—depending on your vital signs. Any weight you gain after that you'll have to gain by eating." He saw the look of alarm that crossed her face. "When you're ready."

It seemed what they had been threatening her with from the very first had finally come true. They had hooked her up to tubes, tubes that kept her chained to the hospital, and now they'd force her to get fat. Kessa was glad her father wasn't there at that moment to savor his triumph.

She lay there for a while thinking of Sandy Sherman's words, vacillating between panic at her loss of control over her body and relief that someone else had finally taken over. And she was glad, too, that it was Sherman who had taken control and not her father. Sherman had never raged against her, and he'd never ignored her either.

"Kessa," Sandy said, "you've got to realize this obsession with weight is not the real problem. Gaining weight isn't really what you're afraid of."

He seemed to be breaking into new territory, and she was frightened. "What do you mean?"

"I know your fear of gaining weight is real, or rather, I know you're really afraid of gaining weight, but that fear is coming from someplace else in your head. It's a question of reality, Kessa. If you had been too fat, then your fear of gaining weight would have been real, but since you almost died of starva-

176

tion, we know there couldn't have really been a chance of your being too fat. So the problem must be something else, and when we find out what it is, you'll be free from this terrible trap."

His words were somehow reassuring, just as they were when he told her things she was feeling even though she hadn't expressed those feelings. For the first time in longer than she could remember, she felt almost safe, but the emotion was followed almost immediately by a resurgent fear.

"I still don't want to gain weight."

"I know you don't, but the idea will become less scary as time goes on."

How did he know the idea of gaining weight was scary? Everyone else just assumed she didn't eat because she didn't want to, but he knew that she couldn't eat because she was terrified to.

"Are you sure of that?" she asked.

"Absolutely positive, Kessa. And remember, I'm in control, so if I say I'm sure, it's so."

After Sandy had left, Kessa lay for a long time staring at the ceiling, still swinging back and forth between fear at her helplessness in the face of her enemy, the bottle, and relief that Sherman had taken control. She began to think about taking care of and being taken care of, and she remembered the day last summer when Susanna had left for California. Kessa hadn't thought of her sister in weeks. She hadn't thought of anything but food and her own fear.

It was a curious group that had stood in front of the prewar apartment house on Central Park West that Sunday morning more than a year ago. Kessa had come down with her parents to say good-bye to Susanna. She could still see the expression on her father's face when the van, a garish hodgepodge of spray-paint flowers and love-and-peace slogans, pulled up. It was an expression Kessa knew well. She saw it on his face practically every time Susanna did anything these days.

Kessa stood a little aside from the group, shifting her weight from one foot to the other while her mother asked about Susanna's plans in California and her father fired questions at the driver about the condition of the van. God, she wished they'd say good-bye and get it over with. But of course they'd want to hold on to Susanna for as long as possible. And of course Susanna would want to hang on to the limelight for as long as she could.

As Kessa stood there on the edge of Susanna's circle of light, she began to run another scene through her mind. She saw herself saying good-bye to her parents, saw her father shrug, her mother tell her to have a good time, and the two of them turn and walk back into the apartment house.

Her mother was hugging Susanna now and crying. Damn it, wouldn't they ever finish? Her father was telling Susanna to come home anytime she wanted; he'd send her the air fare. "And let me know if you need money for anything else." Kessa could hear the embarrassment in his voice. He'd sworn he wouldn't give her another penny after she went to California.

"For *anything*, Daddy?" Susanna teased him.

Kessa wondered how she could do it. An hour ago her sister and father had been at each other's throats, and now Susanna was doing one of her adorable acts, as if her father were some guy she wanted to turn on. Kessa wished her sister would take her adorable ass—her big, sexy, adorable ass—

178

and put it in the van. She'd had enough of the dramatic exit.

Susanna was about to get in when she remembered Francesca. "So long, peanut. Hang in there. And don't look so grim. Maybe you can come visit me next winter. How'd you like that?"

Kessa half nodded, half shrugged in a futile attempt to tell her sister she'd love to come and her parents she wouldn't dream of leaving them.

Then Susanna was gone, and Kessa was alone with her parents. But that night when she went into Susanna's room to see if her sister had left anything interesting, Kessa heard her parents arguing about Susanna again and knew that she wasn't alone with them at all. She was simply alone.

The day after Kessa's surgery Myrna paid another visit. "They got you. I knew they would, especially after I heard that business with your fainting in the middle of the night. They said you almost died." There was an edge of anger to her voice. Myrna, the star anorexic of a handful of hospitals, did not like being upstaged. "Boy, it really freaked me out the first time they put me on hyperal."

"The first time?" Kessa said.

"Yeah, I showed you the marks. I've had three courses—that's what they call it. Once I even pulled it out myself. Boy, did that shake them up."

The image of Myrna tearing the catheter from her flesh made Kessa cringe in imagined pain. "Didn't it hurt?"

"It hurt all right, but at least I got back at them. Showed them it wasn't as easy to make me fat as they thought. I had the whole floor hopping that

179

time. That was in the hospital before the last one."

"How long have you been like this?" Kessa asked.

"Three years, a little more. I told you, kid, I'm a pro. When you feel a little stronger I'll show you how to exercise with that thing."

"Exercise?"

"Sure. I can walk the hall as fast with that thing as I can without it. You'll learn soon enough."

"I don't want to learn," Kessa said, close to tears. Could there really be a resemblance between this crazy, emaciated girl and herself?

"Ha!" Myrna pronounced, and shuffled out of the room.

"You still tryin' to tell me it ain't a game?" Lila said. "She goes through all that shit to have them put it in and then goes ahead and just rips it out. Makes about as much sense as my breaking this cast. And don't think I wouldn't like to sometimes. It itches like a bitch. But I got enough sense to leave it on till my leg gets better. If you ask me, that girl ain't got enough sense to . . ." Lila searched for the thought. " . . . to keep herself alive."

"But I'm not like her."

"Then how come you got that tube comin' out of your neck? You wanna tell me that?"

17

Grace had started to dial the number three times that afternoon. Each time she'd gotten as far as the California area code and hung up. This time she was not going to. *Why shouldn't I call Susanna to talk about Francesca? Why shouldn't I ask her to come to see her sister? After all, Francesca is in the hospital.*

Grace thought without amusement that Harold would be both pleased and chagrined that a boy's voice answered the phone. Susanna's absence, she knew, had not lessened at all Hal's fascination with her.

"Hi, Mom." The girl's voice cut into Grace's thoughts. "What's up?"

Grace dispensed with the niceties. "Kessa's about the same. Still on hyperal—you know, that tube in the chest I wrote you about."

"Ugh. It sounds awful."

"The whole thing is awful." Grace heard the break in her own voice. And she'd sworn she wasn't going to cry.

"Don't, Mom. Everything's going to be all right. You'll see." *Damn, but I wish she wouldn't cry long-distance*, Susanna thought. *What does she expect me to do?*

"I wish I could be as optimistic."

"Well, if you can't *do* anything, there's no point in being anything but optimistic."

"I was wondering, Susanna . . . it's been so long . . ."

Here it comes, thought Susanna. *She's going to ask me to come home.*

"Perhaps you could come home—just for a few weeks." Grace heard the silence and told herself for the hundredth time there was nothing wrong with a mother leaning on a daughter once in a while.

"Oh . . . I guess so. I mean, why not? It's only a few weeks." She figured she owed that much to her mother.

"That's wonderful, just wonderful. I know Francesca's dying to see you. We'll be able to visit her by then."

They talked for a few minutes about plane schedules and Susanna's life.

"Listen, Mom, I have to run. The kids are waiting."

"Sure, you go ahead. We'll see you on Thursday." There was a moment's silence. "And Susanna . . . thank you."

Grace decided to take a different tack with Gregg. He hadn't been bombarded for the past months with letters and phone calls chronicling Francesca's illness. She hadn't thought it fair to bother him—he was involved at Harvard, and now in his summer job at Woods Hole. But after her conversation with Susanna, she decided it was time to remind him that he had a younger sister who was very ill indeed. Not that she rushed into the matter. The letter Grace finally composed was a masterpiece of understatement. Only after she'd inquired about Gregg's work and whether he was enjoying himself on the Cape and related all the cheerful news she could think of did she even broach the subject of Francesca.

You know how I hate to be the bearer of bad news, but I'm afraid Francesca is in the hospital. She was dieting a little too severely, and the doctors thought she was endangering her health. Apparently it's not an uncommon problem among teenage girls. It's called anorexia nervosa. She's at Northeast Hospital so they can monitor her weight and her health, and she's been seeing a psychologist who seems competent. At any rate Francesca seems to like him, and that's what counts.

I know she'd love it if you could get home for a weekend to see her, and I wish you'd give her a call at the hospital. I'm sure she'd love to hear from you.

Grace went on for a few paragraphs. It wouldn't do to end a letter to Gregg on a depressing note.

A few days later he wrote back saying he couldn't possibly get away at the moment but he would call Francesca.

Kessa heard her voice sound small and frightened over the long-distance wire.

"Listen, kiddo," Gregg bounced back, all good-natured confidence, "what's this business about your dieting yourself into the hospital? You don't need a diet, and you can take that from a man of the world who knows what he's talking about."

"I just wanted to lose a few pounds." She returned to the familiar plaint.

"Well, you've got it together now, haven't you?"

"Sure. I'm a little bored here, but they·say I have to gain some more weight before I leave."

"Then gain it and get out of there. Helluva place to spend the summer anyway. What happened to that backpacking trip out West we talked about last fall?"

It was a vague memory to Kessa—less than a vague memory. The girl who'd talked of a backpacking tour with a group of kids had been dead for ages.

"You just start putting on that weight, you hear me? I know you, kiddo. You can do anything you set your mind to. Now, no excuses. Fat and happy and out of the hospital on the double."

Kessa knew he was joking, but she could not help the wave of panic that washed over her at the word *fat*.

"You coming home soon, Gregg?"

"Won't be able to make it for a while, kid. Maybe at the end of the summer for a weekend. We'll see. You get yourself out of that hospital, and then we'll talk about it. Got to run now, Francesca. Remember, start shoveling that food in."

"Son of a bitch," she muttered as she slammed down the receiver.

Lila heard the words and turned from the afternoon soaps she was watching. She was surprised to see Kessa's face contorted in anger.

"What the hell's the matter with you? One

minute you're talkin' on the phone all nice and friendly, the next you're sittin' there makin' faces."

"He's such a pain in the ass."

"Who?"

"My brother. My brother the A-number-one-all-American-pain-in-the-ass."

"Then how come you didn't tell him that? How come you were so nice to him, and now you're sittin' here gettin' angry all by yourself?"

"I couldn't tell him what I really thought."

"Why the hell not?"

"Well, he doesn't want to hear my problems. If I started to tell him I was depressed, he'd just try to get off the phone. And then he wouldn't like me."

"Shit, if my brother didn't like me because I was depressed, tough on him. I ain't puttin' on no act for nobody."

"You don't understand, Lila."

"Seems to me I understand a lot better than you do. Girl, if I'm angry, I scream, and if something hurts, I yell. You ever hear me when the doctor starts messin' around with my foot? Well maybe I make too much noise, but I'll tell you something. Them doctors are always sayin', 'Does it hurt here? Does it hurt here?' and if I don't tell them, they don't know. And if they don't know they'll just go on hurtin' me. And I ain't about to let anyone do that."

"Yeah, but this is different."

"Bullshit. You go on not screamin' and you're just askin' people to keep on hurtin' you."

Myrna took to dropping in several times a day. "Still can't stand up?" she asked on the third day after Kessa's surgery.

"I tried, but I get dizzy."

"It's a shame. You're not getting any exercise. I always like to get exercise when they're pouring that shit into me." Myrna looked gleefully at the bottle hanging from the pole next to Kessa's bed. She had gathered from the doctors and nurses that Kessa was a threat to her superiority. The thought of Kessa trapped in her bed gaining ounce after ounce while Myrna prowled the hall and plied her trade—a sneaked meal here, a secret vomit there—delighted her.

"I'll tell you the truth," Myrna continued. "You had me worried for a while. You see, I'm always the worst. At the last hospital they couldn't believe how bad I was, and there have been three other girls in and out since I've been here, but none of them was as bad as me. But for a while I thought you were going to be."

"Man, I must be in the psycho ward," Lila said.

Myrna ignored the comment from a noninitiate. "I just like to be the worst, that's all. Everybody's got something they like to be better at than anybody else. With me it's anorexia."

"But don't you ever want to go home?" Kessa asked.

"I don't know. Maybe after you do. Anyway I'm a long way from that. I only weigh sixty, and they never let me go home at that. I'm five one. I can get down to fifty-six. Then they put me on hyperal. What were you when they put you on?"

"Sixty-three and a half."

"See, I am the worst. I can walk around lower than anybody else. They would never bother to put me on hyperal at sixty-three and a half. Hell, at sixty-three and a half I'm running around helping the nurses and serving trays and stuff like that. Donaldson can't believe it. When I first came to him I was fifty-three, and he couldn't believe it. He's your doctor too, isn't he?" Myrna asked.

"Yeah, one of them."

"Do you like him?"

"He's all right, I guess."

"Does he like you?" Myrna persisted.

"How do I know? Besides I don't care," she lied. "All I want to do is get out of here."

"Well, I wish you luck," Myrna said on her way out the door.

"Miss Crazy's probably going off to binge or vomit or hide some food in her bed," Lila said, remembering the first conversation she'd overheard between the two skinnies.

Kessa did not answer. She was thinking of her own behavior and hoping Lila hadn't noticed. For the first few days in the hospital, Kessa had been too terrified and disoriented to keep up most of her magical games. She hadn't eaten anything, so there had been no dividing up and parceling out of food. There had been no chanting in time to her name, and though she had continued to observe her bathroom rituals, Lila's constant proximity didn't seem to allow much chance for self-examination or any of the other habits. But a curious thing happened the day they put the hyperal in. When Kessa realized that the tube binding her to the container of liquid also bound her to the hospital, she became more secure there. The rituals had begun again. And they in turn began to strengthen this new feeling of security.

The NPO regime had lasted less than a day, and she had begun to collect the plastic utensils that came with the hospital meals. In her night

187

table drawer she had twenty of them arranged neatly in piles of knives, forks, and spoons. When Lila was wheeled out of the room for something, Kessa would open the drawer and arrange and rearrange her cache. She had also begun to save sugar packets. They lined the drawer like little white sandbags, a line of defense against the dangers that stalked her. And just this afternoon she'd broken new ground. The rituals were an old game to her, but stealing and hoarding food was something new. At home Kessa had thought about food all the time, but she'd never had to lay in secret supplies of it. Now that they watched every mouthful they put before her and checked for bingeing and vomiting, she'd begun to rise to new levels of deception. When they had wheeled Lila out for an examination this afternoon, they had pushed the bed table with her tray on it across the room so it would not be in the way. It sat only inches from Kessa's bed. On the plate a thin film of mashed potatoes had begun to harden. Next to it lay a piece of fatty discarded meat. Quickly, without even thinking, Kessa snatched the plate and put it in the drawer beneath the one with the sugar and utensils. As an afterthought she took Lila's utensils and placed them in the top drawer with the others. When the woman came to take the trays away, she looked carefully at Kessa's but did not even notice that Lila had eaten not only her lunch, but apparently the plate as well.

The incident gave Kessa courage. On the next day she tried a more dangerous ploy. Once again they had wheeled Lila out right after lunch, but today Kessa had her mind on bigger stakes than Lila's leftovers. Kessa had cut her own tuna fish sandwich into quarters and eaten only one of them. She had not opened the container of milk at all.

She put the uneaten sandwich, the container of milk, and a styrofoam container of pudding into the drawer with Lila's food. The unused plastic spoon went in the top drawer with her collection. She'd rearrange them later when she had more time. Then, holding on to the bed, Kessa stood unsteadily, and slid the empty tray under it. She got back into bed and rang for the nurse.

"I never got my lunch," she said when the young nurse came in. Kessa was glad she'd drawn this one. Most of the staff treated her distantly—Myrna had said doctors and nurses didn't like anorexics much—but this young nurse didn't seem to dislike Kessa. "The other nurse helped me to the bathroom. I guess I was in there when they came, and they forgot me."

"Then we'll just have to find you some lunch." The nurse had been on this floor for only a week and knew nothing of the wiles she was up against. It took some time. There were no extra trays on the floor. Finally, she'd gone to another. "All I could come up with," the nurse said, walking into Kessa's room with the fresh tray, "was a tuna salad with potato chips, milk, and jello. How's that sound?"

"Okay, I guess. Thanks a lot."

The nurse put the tray on the bed table and left, feeling pleased that one of the anorexic kids was beginning to eat. Kessa began to divide the salad into four portions, each separated by a small mound of potato chips. *But I won't eat the potato chips*, she told herself. *Just one section of the salad and a quarter of a glass of milk.*

Four days after her surgery Kessa could walk, but she was still unsteady and needed help to navigate anything more ambitious than the route to the bathroom. Myrna would sometimes take her for a stroll down the hall, demonstrating how to move the bottle and pole smoothly. It was obvious that Myrna enjoyed taking care of her, but Kessa knew too that Myrna was still in competition. She didn't want Kessa to walk too much, and after one trip up and down the hall, Myrna would take her back to her room and begin her own more vigorous hiking.

When Kessa returned to her room on the fifth afternoon after surgery, Lila was sitting up in bed making a face. "You smell something funny in here?" The smell of tuna fish and then rotting tuna fish had become so familiar to Kessa that she didn't really smell anything.

"Well, I do and it stinks." Lila hadn't said anything at first because she had thought it might be her own bedpan and was embarrassed, but she had used the bedpan hours ago and the room still stank. "Maybe somebody dropped something. I'm going to call the nurse."

The nurse who arrived was not the young one Kessa had found so easy to fool.

"You're right, Lila," she said. "Something smells awful in here. Like rotting food." The woman looked at Kessa. "Kessa, have you been hiding food?"

"No."

"Then I guess we'll have to do a search. Maybe someone dropped something from a tray and the cleaning men missed it."

The nurse performed a cursory search around Lila's bed. When she crossed to Kessa's side of the room, she became more thorough. It took her less than a minute to locate the pilfered lunch and Lila's leftovers. "You know this is against the rules, Kessa."

"Rules, that's all you ever talk about. The rules

are stupid. First you tell me you want me to gain weight, then when I put aside some food in case I get hungry later . . ."

"Kessa, this food is days old. If you tried to eat it, you'd be sick as a dog. You know if you want a snack you can ask for it."

"What if I don't want to ask for it? What if I don't want to go begging every time I feel like eating something? Don't I have any rights around here?" She was screaming now, and the tears had begun to run down her face. "This place is a prison, a goddamn prison, and you treat me like a goddamn prisoner. I don't have any rights at all."

"Your rights, Kessa, have nothing to do with keeping you alive, and that's what we're trying to do." The nurse's voice sounded strangely calm and quiet after Kessa's outburst. "It's perfectly true our rules infringe on your freedom and your privacy and maybe even your rights, Kessa, but if we let you have all the freedom and privacy and rights you want, you'd starve yourself to death. And if you're dead, what good are freedom and privacy and rights going to do you?"

Kessa said nothing, but the expression on her face told the nurse she had backed down.

"By breaking the rules, Kessa," the nurse continued, "you've proved you can't be trusted. Now, after every meal, one of the nurses will search your bed, night table, closet, and any other place you might hide food. I'm not trying to frighten you, but I think I ought to warn you that when this happens a second or third time the punishments are generally harsher. I've seen patients confined to their beds and telephones disconnected because of hoarding or vomiting. That's not a threat, Kessa, just a warning about the way we run things here."

"Old bitch," Kessa muttered when the nurse had left the room, but there was no force to the words. She felt beaten. Kessa turned over and buried her face in the pillow. She would not look at Lila. Lila had caught her, had seen the hidden meal, and worse, the revolting remains of her own, and now she thought she was as crazy as Myrna—and as disgusting.

"You know, Kessa, you're lookin' a lot better." Lila's disgust with Kessa for the cache of rotting food had passed, and now she felt sorry for her. Kessa was crazy, but at least she wasn't as bad as Myrna. "Since they stuck that thing in you and you're up and walkin' around, you look a lot better. Hey, what's buggin' you anyhow? I tell you you look better and you get this attitude like I insulted you."

"I didn't mean it, Lila. I just got a pain in my shoulder. Sometimes this thing still bothers me."

"Bullshit. You don't want to look better."

"I like the way I look now."

"You like lookin' like a zebra?"

"What do you mean?"

"Girl, you got so many veins stickin' through your skin, you look striped." Lila didn't dare to mention the truly repulsive part of Kessa's appearance. Usually she kept herself wrapped up in a long-sleeved robe or a sweater—she said she was always cold—but a couple of times when Lila had seen her in just the hospital-issue gown, she was shocked by the hair that covered Kessa's body.

"Well, I still like the way I look," Kessa insisted.

"All I can say is, if you like the way you look

now, maybe there's something wrong with your eyes instead of your head."

Of course Myrna had heard about the incident of the hidden food. "You're learning, Kessa, but not fast enough. You have to be careful what you take and how long you keep it. Once it starts smelling, you're in trouble. I would've binged right away."

"And then thrown it up?" Kessa did not try to keep the disgust from her voice.

"Little Miss Holier-Than-Thou. What were you planning on doing with that crap if not bingeing and then throwing it up? You think I'm crazy because I want to be the worst anorexic around. Well, at least I know what I am. But you're so sick you can't even recognize what you are." The idea that Kessa's refusal to see her own illness might make her the sickest of all alarmed Myrna. "Or maybe you're just dumb," she added, and left the room quickly.

18

Kessa still found it difficult to walk without aid. Sandy usually came to her room and helped her along to the office where they met. The three of them inched their way down the hospital corridor now—an emaciated, grim-looking child helped by a tall, bearded man, and a pole supporting the fluid that kept the girl alive. Sherman had made a habit of teasing Kessa about the three of them, but his mind's eye told him they did not make a funny picture.

When they reached the office and he lowered her gently into an armchair, he saw how much effort this short walk had cost her.

"How are you feeling?" he asked.

"Bored."

"And still weak?"

"Kind of," she admitted. Her attempt to hide her condition depressed him further. "And like a freak," she blurted out, and began to cry. "I don't belong here." Kessa thought of the ease with which Lila talked and kidded with the other girls on the floor and remembered how wary and sometimes disapproving she'd become with Kessa. "I'm in the hospital, but I'm not really sick."

"You are sick, Kessa. You almost died." And you're not out of the woods yet, he wanted to add, but did not.

"Oh, it's not just the hospital. It's everything. I never fit in." She remembered that the harder she'd tried to please Madame in dance class, the more she'd felt the other girls were laughing at her. She recalled the party she'd gone to with Julia last spring. "I never fit in anywhere," she repeated through the tears. "At parties, with other kids, never . . ."

"I guess since in your head you don't feel as if you belong, you end up not feeling as if you belong wherever you are."

"No, no, no." It was a wail. "I really don't belong. Everyone else belonged, but not me."

Sandy suddenly realized the breakthrough he was waiting for had come. Perhaps the stay at the hospital, and all the pain and fatigue of the past days, had somehow made her more accepting of his support. He needed to keep this discussion going.

"What about at home? Didn't you feel as if you belonged there?"

"Home! That was the worst of all. *She* always belonged. Oh, she could do whatever she wanted. She pulled more shit than you could imagine, drove them crazy half the time, but *she* still belonged."

"Who's *she*, Kessa?"

"Susanna. Big, blond, sexy, noisy, come-out-fighting Susanna. Why the hell did I have to have a sister like that? Why the hell did I have to have a sister?" Kessa was crying so hard now Sherman could barely understand the words. He took a tissue from the box on the desk and wiped her eyes and

196

face. Then he handed her another, and she blew her nose.

"And *he* belonged too. Oh, God, did he belong. Nobody ever belonged like old Gregory Dietrich. Mr. Perfect. Everything he did was perfect. Everything he said was perfect. He even looked perfect. Well, I'll tell you something about my goddamn perfect brother. Just come to him with a problem and he picks up that perfect ass of his and runs like shit. But the best part is, all the time he's running, he's smiling at you—that perfect Gregg Dietrich smile that says, 'it may look like I'm running, but I'm not really running at all, because after all, how could somebody as perfect as I am run?'"

"So you didn't belong at school and you didn't belong at home. But you must have had friends."

"Maybe I used to. I don't anymore."

"Well, when you did have friends, Kessa, when you were with groups of kids your own age, did you have the same feeling about not belonging with them as you did with your family?"

"That's what I've been telling you." She began to cry again. "I never belonged."

"Isn't it possible that's only what you felt?"

"What do you mean?"

"Some of us have feelings that remain the same even though the situations change. So it's the feeling of not belonging that we're talking about, not the actual condition of not belonging. I'm asking if maybe you carry that feeling around in you all the time, just ready to call on it when necessary. And then, because you've got this feeling of not belonging, you figure it's hopeless to try. I mean, you've already got the I-don't-belong feeling in your head, so why bother trying?"

"Yeah, that's right. Why bother trying? It's hopeless. It's worse than that."

Though his manner remained calm, Sherman's mind was racing. He was thinking of the obsessions he'd discovered in the other two anorexics he was treating and remembering half-forgotten sentences and paragraphs from years of reading. It would be a risk pushing her this way, but he had gambled that day when he'd raced from room to room, and he'd won. Sandy decided it was time to gamble again.

"Now, tell me something, Kessa. If you think there's no point in trying, if you think that people aren't going to let you belong no matter what you do, then what do you do? How do you behave to them?"

"What do you mean?" The misery in her voice had turned to defensiveness. Sherman was fairly sure the game was going to payoff.

"Isn't it possible," he asked, "that since you expect them to reject you, you reject them first? That since you expect them not to let you belong, to be mean to you, you're mean to them first?"

"Now you're doing it. Now you're saying I'm not a nice person. You're saying I'm mean."

"I'm not saying anything of the sort, Kessa. I'm saying maybe you're so worried about not belonging that you send out messages saying you don't want to belong."

"Well, what would you do? Sit around and wait for them to come out and tell you 'go away, we hate you'?"

"I think I'd probably do just what you're doing." Sherman held his breath for a moment. Then he turned over his cards. "I think I'd find a whole lot of things to do that would make me feel better about it. Like little magical tricks that would protect me from them and from not belonging or might even make me belong."

She looked at him suspiciously. "What kind of things?"

"Maybe I'd make up magical games that would control the way people felt toward me. I might make bets with myself. Like if I can walk to the corner before the light changes, so-and-so will like me. Or if I arrange everything in my room in a certain order, I'll belong to a certain group. Or"—his voice did not change, but Sherman was holding his breath —"if I cut up my food in a certain way or only eat certain things or don't eat certain things, I might protect myself from other people's bad feelings. I can think of a whole bunch of rituals or special tricks that might protect me from anything that might go wrong in my life. Of course, then I'd run the risk of falling into a bad trap."

"What kind of a bad trap?"

"Well, if I started using these tricks to make me safe, I'd probably keep adding to them to make me more and more safe, and the more tricks I'd have, the more time I'd have to spend on them. I might begin to forget why I was doing a certain trick, but I'd know I couldn't stop doing it because then I wouldn't be safe anymore. And there would be more and more tricks and less and less time to do them, and pretty soon all my life would be tricks—that, and the terrified feeling I'd have if I missed one."

She was silent for what seemed to Sherman a very long time. When she finally spoke, she kept her eyes on the floor and her voice was so low he could barely hear her.

"I have tricks. I . . . have . . . lots . . . and . . . lots . . . of . . . magic . . . tricks. My life *is* magic tricks."

Sherman's voice was full of sympathy, but he felt as if he'd just broken the bank at Monte Carlo. "That doesn't sound very pleasant."

"It's awful. It's terrifying."

"Do you want to stop them, Kessa? Do you want to get rid of the magical tricks?"

"I can't. I've tried, but I can't."

"You can, Kessa—if you want to."

"How?"

"You have to begin by telling me. If you share the rituals with me, you'll be betraying them. And that's the beginning of getting rid of them."

"But there are so many of them."

"We have plenty of time."

"And they're so embarrassing. You'll think I'm crazy. You'll think I'm awful."

"I promise you I won't think any of those things. But you're going to have to tell me, Kessa. There's no other way."

"Will that really stop them?"

"Eventually."

She was suspicious again. "What do you mean, eventually?"

"If I told you they'd go away tomorrow, I'd be lying. And I think you're just using this time business as an excuse not to tell me."

"But it's so hard." The tears were flowing again. "So hard . . ."

"I know that, Kessa. I know that when we talk about these things, it's much easier for me than it is for you. Everything we're going to say and do is going to be harder for you than for me, but that

200

isn't going to stop me from pushing you. I'm going to push you to say whatever has to be said and to do whatever has to be done. The fact that I'm going to push you doesn't mean I don't understand how painful it is for you, but it does mean I know you're strong enough to do it."

"Maybe I'm not as strong as you think," she countered.

"And maybe you're looking for an excuse not to tell me the tricks because you're scared to tell me the tricks."

"Aren't I even allowed to be scared?"

"Of course you're allowed to be scared, but it won't stop me from pushing you. Kessa, I think there's a part of you that wants to get rid of those rituals desperately, desperately enough to tell me about them. But another part of you is too frightened to tell me."

"You make it sound like a war."

"Isn't it?"

"I guess so." She was silent for a moment. "Do we have to talk about them now?"

"We have to start now."

Sherman watched her through another long silence. When she finally spoke, her voice was thick with misery.

"Shit, this is hard."

"I know it's hard, Kessa, but it's the only way."

"Well, there are a lot of crazy things. Some are about food and some are about . . . other things."

"Why don't you tell me one of the food ones first?"

"I'm not supposed to put the whole fork in my mouth. Only up to the tines. And my lips can't touch it. I have to get the food off the fork without my lips touching it."

"Yes?"

"Well, don't you see? Food might collect between the tines. It might get on my lips." She stopped and waited for him to speak.

"I understand."

"But what do you think?"

"I think you should tell me some more."

"Well, another thing is that I always have to decide what part of a meal I won't eat before I begin eating."

Again she waited for a response, and again there was none. He didn't laugh, he didn't smile, he didn't even look surprised.

"There's always one part of the meal I can't eat at all." She spoke slowly, haltingly. "Like the potatoes at dinner. And then I have to divide the rest of the meal into parts, like cut up the meat into a certain number of pieces and arrange those in equal parts or divide a sandwich in quarters or something like that. Then I'll only eat a certain number of them." There was still no response from Sherman. "And in a restaurant, the price counts."

"What do you mean?"

"Well, it ought to be divisible by four. Like if a sandwich costs a dollar sixty, I can order it. But then I still have to divide it into fours." She was silent for a while.

"Are there other rituals, Kessa? Tricks that have nothing to do with food?"

"I have to have everything arranged in certain ways. At home I kept all my clothes in a certain order. If a skirt wasn't in its right place, I'd have to rearrange the closet. And here there's a certain order for everything in my drawers."

"Anything else?"

"Not really."

"I think there must be." His voice was gentle but firm.

"Well, there are some bathroom things."

"Go on, Kessa."

"I can't sit down on the toilet seat. You know, like you're not supposed to in public places. Well, I can't anywhere. Not here, not even at home."

"Are there any more?" Sherman prodded, and this time she answered more easily. She had told the worst—the food and the bathroom—and now she listed a host of rules about the way the covers on her bed must be folded, the knee socks in her drawer rolled, the things on her desk arranged.

"It sounds as if you're pretty busy. In fact, it sounds as if you don't have time for anything else except your rituals. You're a slave to them, Kessa."

"I guess I am, but I can't stop doing them."

"Why not?"

"It'd be too dangerous. I wouldn't be able to. I mean, you could forbid me to do them, but it wouldn't do any good. I have to keep doing them."

"I know you do, Kessa—for the moment. And I'm not going to forbid you to do them. I think perhaps we'll try to deal with them in another way."

"What do you mean?" She was suspicious again.

"Well, you just told me about them, right? And most of them had to do with food. So I think Thursday I'll come early, and we'll have lunch together. That way you won't just talk about them with me, you'll do them with me."

"You're kidding. I couldn't. I just couldn't."

"You said the same thing about talking about them, but you just did that."

"But that would be worse, much worse. I'd never be able to."

"Kessa, an hour ago you thought you weren't strong enough to tell me about your tricks. I said you were. And I turned out to be right, didn't I? You told me about the rituals and nothing terrible has happened. Well, now I'm telling you you're strong enough to do the rituals with me, and not only is nothing terrible going to happen to you, but it's going to be the beginning—remember, I said only the beginning—of getting rid of them. That's why you have to do them with me, and you *can* do them with me."

There was nothing harsh in his voice, but she knew he wasn't giving her a choice. He was saying he knew she could do something, and she was going to do it no matter how much it frightened her. He didn't argue, he didn't negotiate; he simply told her what he knew she was capable of. And for a moment Kessa almost believed it herself.

But when Sherman was gone and Kessa was left alone with her fears, eating lunch with him was no longer a possibility. It became something to avoid at all costs.

He had told her at her first appointment that she could always call him in his office at ten of the hour, and if he was not there and she felt it was an emergency she could call him at home. Yet the only time Kessa had called Sherman was when Dr. Gordon had told her she was to be hospitalized. Now, for the next forty-eight hours, Kessa bombarded him with calls. She had a hundred reasons for not being able to eat in front of him.

"Listen, Kessa," he said finally, "if an experience is frightening to you, I'd like to share that experience. I think that in many ways you exist alone. I'd like to change that." Again his tone was at once so kind and authoritative that she was left without an argument.

19

Sherman arrived a little before noon on Thursday. He had arranged for them to have their trays in the small office where they usually met, and as he helped Kessa down the hall he could feel her trembling. He eased her into a chair, then went out to get their trays. Left alone in the office, Kessa raced through her rituals frantically. She had no idea what was for lunch, but she had to make a decision now. She wouldn't possibly be able to decide what to eat and what to leave over in front of him. She heard him in the outer office and decided that if there was a vegetable, she wouldn't eat it. Everything else would be divided into fourths.

Kessa was almost relieved when she saw Sherman enter with two trays. She prayed he'd be distracted by his own lunch but knew he would not.

As if he had read her mind, Sandy sat down and busied himself with his food. He took the metal dome from the plate. "The old hospital standby," he said. "Salisbury steak. Well, a hamburger by any other name is still a hamburger." On each tray was a can of tomato juice. He began to pull the tab off his. "These tabs are stiff. Would you like me to open yours?"

"No thanks, I can do my own." She picked up the can of juice and started to pull, but the familiar pain shot down her arm.

Sherman saw the tears welling up in her eyes and reached over to help her. He put his left hand over hers on the can and pulled the tab with his right; then he began to eat. While he ate, Kessa fidgeted. She opened the napkin and placed it carefully on her lap. She unwrapped the small square of butter and brushed it back and forth, back and forth across the mashed potatoes. She poured the tomato juice exactly halfway up the cup. She cut the hamburger into four equal portions, then divided three of them in half and those halves in half again. She moved the food around the plate. Sherman had finished his lunch, and Kessa still had not put a morsel in her mouth.

"I just feel so scared," she finally broke out. "I was going to say the food was too cold, but that's not true. It's not the food, it's me. I'm terrified."

"What are you terrified of, Kessa?"

"That I'm going to eat too much and I'll get too fat. And this awful tube makes it worse. If I don't eat at all, it's still pouring calories into me."

"Even if you didn't have the tube, you'd feel frightened, wouldn't you?" Sherman asked.

"I guess so."

"So you must be afraid of something besides eating or gaining weight."

"What do you mean?"

"It's very possible to have a reasonable fear of gaining too much weight, Kessa, but when you've lost so much weight that you've almost died, then the fear of being too fat can't possibly be reasonable. A reasonable fear is one that disappears when the danger disappears. In this case the danger disappeared so entirely that your life was in danger, but you were still afraid. That's why I think you're afraid of something else besides being fat. You see, you only tell yourself you're afraid of gaining too much weight because you're more comfortable being afraid of that than of what really frightens you."

Kessa looked down at her food, then back at Sherman. Her eyes were full of confusion and misery.

"I guess," he continued, "that I just can't believe you're as frightened of that plate of food as you want me to believe you are. I'm not suggesting you're faking, but I am suggesting that a part of you finds it easier to believe that food is more dangerous than something else." He took her fork, flattened out the mound of mashed potatoes, and sketched a frown-face in it. "Boo! I'm going to eat you up."

Almost against her will, she giggled.

"Now look at yourself in the mirror."

She was startled. He led her to the mirror on the back of the office door and lifted her arm by the elbow. "About this arm, would you say it's too heavy, just right, or too thin?"

"Somewhere between just right and too thin," Kessa said.

"And if we asked for ten unbiased opinions about this arm, what do you think they'd be?"

"Too thin?"

"Why do you think they'd think that?"

"I know what you want me to say. You want me to say they'd think that because I am too thin."

"Then if you are too thin and everyone else sees it, why don't you?"

"Because I'm crazy. All right. I said it. I'm crazy. Now are you happy?"

"Do you know what crazy means, Kessa?"

"Screwed up, nuts, bonkers! Okay?"

"Crazy means your feelings aren't working right. Crazy means your head is playing tricks on you, giving you false information about yourself and false fears that can never be allayed because they are false." He led her from the mirror back to the chair. "It's our job, Kessa, to find out what the real fears are. When we can identify those fears, maybe we'll be able to allay them."

She picked up the fork and mashed out the frown face in the potatoes. "I think I can eat some of this now."

"I only want you to eat half, at the most."

"I probably won't eat that much."

"That's okay, but half is the limit."

When Sherman reached his office, he took Kessa's file from the cabinet and jotted down a few notes: "Joined resistance. Took initiative with obsessive rules relating to eating. Visible relaxation on Kessa's part followed."

Kessa had fallen asleep after lunch, but at four-thirty she awoke with a start. Something was wrong, terribly wrong. She didn't know what it was, but she knew something awful was going to happen, and there was nothing she could do to prevent it. Without looking at her watch, she dialed Sherman's number.

"I'm sorry, Kessa, I'm in session now. I'll call you back at ten of five." He didn't sound angry, but he did sound firm.

She lay on her bed staring at the ceiling and feeling the tears run down her face into her hair. She'd never make it till ten of five, never.

"Hey, what's wrong with you?" Lila called across the room. "You seemed okay when you came back from seeing that doctor."

"I just wish he'd call back."

"Didn't he say he would?"

"You don't understand. I can't wait. I'm too scared."

"Ain't nothin' to be scared of as far as I can see. He said he'll call back. All you gotta do is lie there and wait. Ain't nothin' gonna happen to you that way."

"You don't understand."

"You said it that time, girl. I don't understand nohow."

Kessa picked up the phone before the first ring had ended. "I'm just so scared," she began to cry into the phone. "I ate all that food and"—she ran a hand experimentally over her stomach—"I can feel it there, making me fatter and fatter, and I'm just so scared."

"Kessa, you didn't eat 'all that food.' I couldn't stay alive eating what you ate for lunch. Neither could you, for that matter."

"You don't understand. I'm just so scared."

"I promise you that you're not going to get fat from that meal."

"Part of me believes you, or at least it wants to believe you, but part of me is so scared."

"Then I guess we're just going to have to work at strengthening the part that believes me and getting rid of the other part."

She liked the way he talked about the two of them doing battle together against something beyond her. "Can I call you again if I get scared?"

"Sure—providing it's ten of the hour."

"So that's what you were so scared of," Lila said when Kessa had hung up the phone. "He made you eat."

"He did not! He doesn't *make* me do anything."

"Have it your way." Lila shrugged her shoulders and turned back to the television.

Kessa continued to lie on her back staring at the ceiling, but the tears had stopped. She thought about Sherman and how much better he'd made her feel. He was so understanding. She tried to picture what it would be like to be his daughter. Did he yell at his children? Kessa thought of her own father. Relying on her own father, being close to him, had always seemed so dangerous, but she wasn't at all afraid to rely on Sandy. It would be wonderful if he were her father. She could trust him and turn to him, and she'd never feel alone or like an outsider again.

Kessa remembered the old game of Queen Francesca Louise and decided to demote herself to princess. That way Sherman could be her father, the king. She hadn't played with the fantasy in a long time, but now it came back in a new form with new force. It was a snowy kingdom, cold and unforgiving, beset by dangers on all sides, but Princess Kessa lived in a warm castle. The walls of the castle were thick and safe, and it was surrounded by a moat that no one could cross unless Princess Kessa allowed them to. She was safe inside her castle because her father, the king, kept her that way, and her safety and her father were the envy of all the realm. Wars raged throughout the land, but Princess Kessa could not hear the guns. Storms ravaged the countryside, but Princess Kessa did not feel the wind. Sometimes she stood in her window framed by the heavy velvet drapes and looked out at the horrors that seethed around the castle. Sometimes she walked from room to room admiring the tapestries of herself with her father, the king. One day she sent a messenger to Sherman asking if they were in danger. The messenger returned from the king with a scroll. On it was written, "Of course not. You're safe as long as you live in my castle."

Kessa lay there spinning the dream, embroidering and elaborating until she felt warmer than she had in months. The warmth reminded her of the way she'd felt when she used to play Queen Francesca Louise. She was warm and safe and happy. She belonged.

Soon the noise of the wagons carrying the dinner trays began to echo down the hall. Kessa looked up at the bottle that hung next to her bed. She ran her hands along her stomach and up to her ribs. She had gained weight. She was sure of it. The warmth was gone and the icy fear had returned. She tried to think of her father, the king, and she felt warm for a moment, but she could not shut out the sight of the bottle pouring nourishment into her. Kessa was on a pendulum. As the hours and days passed, it swung back and forth from the terrible, chilling storm clouds to the warm security of her castle—back and forth, back and forth, back and forth.

20

"Did you hear about crazy Myrna?" Lila asked the next day. "I was wonderin' why she hadn't been snoopin' around here for a while."

"What happened to her?" People were always telling Kessa she had almost died, but she couldn't believe it. Maybe they were right. Maybe Myrna had died.

"They won't let her out of bed. She stole a whole bunch of some kind of sticks or somethin'—the nurse said they call them oxygen catheters—so she could stick them down her throat to vomit. Guess her finger just wasn't workin' no more. One of the nurses found her vomitin' up a storm with one of them. Then she found the whole drawerful. So they took Myrna's phone away, and they're makin' her stay in bed for a week. Well, at least it keeps her out of here. I can't stand hearin' her talk about all them crazy things she does."

"It is pretty disgusting," Kessa agreed, and tried not to think of the container of chocolate pudding she'd swiped last night and put in her drawer. She wasn't really going to eat it, Kessa reassured herself, but it made her feel better to know it was there. That way if she was too scared

215

to eat supper, she could always have a little of it in the middle of the night. No more than a spoonful or two, of course. She wasn't going to get like Myrna and start bingeing and vomiting.

At two o'clock the following morning Kessa awoke with a start. The pendulum had swung to the other extreme, and the winds were howling about her. The warmth and protection of the castle were gone. She thought of calling Sherman, but of course she couldn't call him at this hour. Then it came back to her. She didn't want to call Sherman. She hated Sherman. He'd told her that afternoon that they were going to meet with her family. She'd begun to cry immediately.

"Don't you want to see your family, Kessa?" If anyone else had asked the question, she thought, it would have been an accusation, but Sandy was really asking her whether or not she wanted to see them.

"They can come visit me if they want, but I don't want them to come to one of our meetings."

"Why not?"

What could she tell him? That if she had to sit in the same room with him and her father it would ruin her fantasy about being his daughter? That by sharing Sherman for even an hour she thought she'd be losing him forever? He'd go over to their side, and once again she wouldn't belong.

"Maybe you won't think I'm so nice if you see me with them."

"I doubt that's going to happen, but I do want to see how you react to your parents and sister and how they react . . ."

"My sister! Susanna's coming too?" She could see the entire meeting as if it had already taken place. Susanna would steal the whole show—including Sandy.

"She's home from California, and she's agreed to come. I asked if your brother would come too, but apparently he can't get away."

"Typical."

"Listen, Kessa, I'm not going to stop liking you no matter what happens at this meeting, and we're still going to go on having our own meetings. But I think it would be helpful for all of us to get together, at least this once."

"Could I see you alone just before?"

"If you like."

"And for little bit after?"

"Sure."

She had agreed to the meeting on the basis of those promises, but now, at two in the morning, the old fears were stalking her again. Something dangerous was about to happen. Kessa began to think about the day after tomorrow. The meeting wasn't until two. How would she get through till then? She began to plan her meals. Half the orange juice. The toast divided into halves, then quarters. She'd eat one quarter. She wished it was breakfast time now. She was starving. Kessa remembered dinner. She had separated the chicken croquette into fourths, then into eights, and eaten two of the small sections. She was glad she hadn't eaten more, but her stomach, terribly stretched, it seemed to her, by that huge meal she'd eaten with Sherman, demanded more. Then she remembered the pilfered pudding. Without making a sound, she opened the drawer and took the pudding and a plastic spoon from her growing cache. She would eat half of each of four spoonfuls. Carefully, making sure that her lips did not touch the plastic utensil, she took the chocolate

217

pudding from the spoon with her teeth. If Kessa had had a sense of taste left, she would have noticed that the pudding was peculiar, but her rituals left no room for the nuances of flavor.

Two hours later Kessa awoke with terrible cramps. For half an hour she tossed and turned in the bed trying to find a comfortable position. There was none. For the next half hour she sat in the bathroom feeling as if she were losing her insides. Finally she rang for a nurse, then cursed herself when the one who had found the stolen meal a week ago entered the room. It didn't take long for her to discover the cause of Kessa's illness—or the half-eaten container of pudding. After giving Kessa something for her stomach, the nurse left the room promising that Kessa's doctor would be informed and punishment would follow. Kessa's only comfort as she lay on her side clutching her stomach and wondering what they would do to her was that Lila had slept through the incident.

It was the first conference Sherman had scheduled with the house staff. Donaldson had organized it.

"We've worked with a lot of these kids, and medically we're okay, but from a psychiatric point of view I don't think the program's much of a success."

"You mean you think we can't do any more than just keep them alive?" Sherman asked, remembering one of their early phone calls when Donaldson had suggested that they couldn't cure anorexics, only manage them.

"I don't know. I'm still reserving judgment on that issue, but I do think the staff could use a few pointers on dealing with these kids. You know the story as well as I do, Sandy. The kids are antagonistic and the staff gets hostile. And then there's the manipulation. You know the other anorexic on the floor, Myrna? Yesterday she actually convinced two interns not to take her blood because she'd had a blood test two days ago and it was okay. You should hear her spout out those levels—electrolytes, potassium, chloride, BUN, bilirubin, white count, everything—and she gave the normal values for each to make her point. She's a real pro."

Sherman met with the staff gladly, if a little nervously. At the end of the meeting an intern approached him. The young man had little patience with psychiatry and none at all with psychologists. "Doesn't everything you've said"—the young man's tone was belligerent—"fly in the face of traditional psychiatric practice. Whatever that is," he added pointedly. "Taking the kids over, telling them you're in charge of their lives, touching them, hugging them, getting involved with them." He said the last as if it were an unspeakably filthy thing to do.

Sherman had answered briefly. He knew the intern was more interested in scoring a point than in hearing any answer, but in the elevator on the way to the lobby he was mulling over the problem himself. Nurturing Kessa—that's what he'd come to call it to himself—was one thing, but losing his own professional distance was another. And of course he had lost his professional distance. Why else would he have felt so crestfallen at what she'd done last night? He'd been practicing long enough to know treatment did not move along a linear path. Two steps forward, one step back—or more dispiriting, one step forward, two steps back. He'd seen it happen again and again. Then why had he gotten so upset about Kessa's theft of the pudding? Because he'd gotten too involved with Kessa. Sherman thought of the intern who'd questioned him after the meeting. He still believed he was right. These kids needed to be taken over, to be held and touched and supported and—damn it—nurtured. The trick was to take them over without letting them take you over.

As Sherman walked into his office, the phone was ringing. It was Kessa. Since he'd been at the hospital for the staff meeting, he'd eaten lunch with her. Now she was in a panic about it.

"Why did you let me eat so much?" she wailed.

As he repeated the familiar litany of reassurance, Donaldson's words rang in his head like a death knell. *We can't cure them; the most we can hope for is a lifetime of management*.

21

Grace drove out to the airport alone to pick up Susanna. On the way back home they talked entirely about Francesca. Relieved to have a confidant, Grace poured out the whole grim story, from Dr. Gordon's first pronouncement to their final banishment from the hospital for a month.

"We're going to see her tomorrow for the first time. That's another reason I'm glad you're here. The doctor wants to have a family session. I was glad you said you'd come."

"What about Gregg?"

"Oh, he can't possibly get down from Woods Hole."

"Naturally," Susanna said. "I mean, Gregg isn't a part of our family anymore, is he?"

When Harold came home that night, the two of them were still talking.

"Well, well," he said, "the return of the prodigal daughter." Damn, he thought, I didn't mean to phrase it quite that way. "How was California?"

"California *is* terrific."

"Glad to hear it," he forced himself to say. "Would you like a drink before dinner?"

"Maybe a glass of wine."

Harold poured some wine for Susanna and two scotches for Grace and himself.

"I guess things haven't been so terrific around here," she said, taking the drink from him. "Mommy told me most of it in the car."

"It's been awful. And it's probably harder on your mother than me. At least I go to the office and get lost in those problems eight hours a day."

"It hasn't been any harder on me than it has on you, Hal," Grace said, entering the living room.

Susanna couldn't help thinking that whatever was wrong with her sister, it seemed to have forged a new bond between her parents.

"I just can't understand why," Hal said. "I mean, why Francesca? Of all the children for this to happen to . . ."

"You mean," Susanna cut in, "if there was any justice, it would have happened to me."

Here we go again, thought Grace—and so soon.

"That's not what your father said."

"But it's what he meant. 'Francesca's always been such a good kid.' Read: 'we've always had trouble with Susanna.' Even the way he said hello to me. He can't stand the idea of my living my own life."

"When you can support yourself, Susanna, then you can talk about living your own life," Harold shot back.

"I can support myself. I don't want your damn money."

"But you keep cashing the checks. You're supporting those friends of yours, aren't you?" Harold was standing.

222

"But if I used it to buy an expensive dress or something that would be all right."

"Maybe you'd look better than in that damn Mexican getup you're wearing."

"Everybody in California wears these."

"Only you're not in California."

"I wish I was. I wish I'd never come home."

"Then go back," Harold shouted. "Go back to your commune and get the hell out of here." The two women heard the door to the master bedroom slam behind him.

"Well, it looks like I'm home," Susanna said.

Grace was silent.

"Aren't you going to say anything?"

"I was just thinking, Susanna. About Francesca, not about you. We started out talking about her, but we ended up fighting about you."

"That's the story of my life."

"It's the story of your sister's life too. Maybe that's what's wrong."

22

Kessa was sitting on the end of her bed sulking when Sherman arrived the next day. She did not answer his greeting.

"So, it's sulk time, eh?"

"Well, I really don't want to go through with this. The whole thing was your idea."

"You're right. It was my idea."

"And I'm supposed to like it?"

"Not necessarily."

The two of them walked down the hall to the office where the rest of the Dietrichs were waiting. Sherman introduced himself to the three of them.

"I see you've got a beard like you're supposed to," Hal said.

"Can't graduate without it," Sherman laughed.

It had been a test, and Harold felt slightly relieved that Sherman had passed. Dr. Smith was still fresh in his mind. "Does it matter who we sit next to?"

"Probably."

Harold had been joking again, but Sherman's answer discomfited him.

"I thought we'd all meet together," Sherman

225

began, "because I want to understand how you deal with each other. In other words, I'd like to eavesdrop. You see, when one member of a family shows severe symptoms of hurting emotionally, it often upsets the rest of the family and intensifies conflicts already present. One of the things I'd like to do is explore those conflicts and how they're being intensified by Kessa's illness."

"Kessa?" Susanna asked.

"That's how your sister introduced herself to me."

Three heads turned to Kessa, but she kept her eyes on the mottled gray linoleum.

"Well, I guess changing your name is good for a start," Susanna observed, "if you're planning on changing your personality."

"What do you mean?" Sherman asked.

"I mean, until now Francesca has always been the good one in the family. Correction: she's always been one of the two good ones in the family. She and Gregg were regular angels. And I'm the bad kid."

Sherman looked at Harold and Grace. "Is that true?"

"Of course it's not true," Hal said quickly. "We have no bad kids in our family."

Sandy saw the anger flicker across Susanna's face. He had hoped that this session would clarify the family's emotional dynamics. "You seem angry at your father's defense of you, Susanna."

"He wasn't defending me. 'There are no bad kids in our family because I'm such a sterling father,'" Susanna mimicked Harold's voice. "Last night there was a bad kid in our family, all right."

"I never said you were a bad kid, Susanna."

"Like hell you didn't. You've said nothing else

for as long as I can remember. You've always made me feel like I was no good. At least the kids in the commune thought I was worth something."

Harold stared at the ceiling.

"Mr. Dietrich," Sherman asked, "how do you feel about what Susanna just said?"

"I guess I'm angry. Yes, angry. I've worked all my life to give her and Francesca and Gregg everything. And I'm not talking only about material things. I wanted her to turn out to be a good kid. What's so terrible about a father wanting the best for his kid?"

"Maybe what you think is best for me isn't what I think is best for me," Susanna said.

"Well, I can't see where this is getting us." Harold turned to Sherman. "I mean, I thought we were here because Francesca's sick."

"Don't you think it's possible, Mr. Dietrich, that both you and Susanna could be right?" Sherman turned to Grace. "Mrs. Dietrich, do you and your husband always agree?"

"Of course not. There are a lot of things we see from different points of view."

"That doesn't mean we have a bad marriage," Harold broke in..

"Of course it doesn't, Harold," Grace snapped. "Stop worrying about how we look to Dr. Sherman, and listen. The point is that each of us can look at things differently and it's still all right. We don't have to agree about everything. And you and Susanna don't have to agree about everything."

"But she's wrong," Harold said.

Susanna threw her hands up in disgust. "How can you be so stupid? How can you not see that someone else can have an opinion that's right for them even if it isn't for you?"

"Is this the way you usually get along?" Sherman asked.

"Exactly," Grace answered.

"And where does Kessa come in?" Sherman asked.

All three Dietrichs looked surprised. "What do you mean?" Harold said. "This had nothing to do with Francesca. I guess that's why I can't understand her being sick. She never gets involved in these battles."

"When we started, Mr. Dietrich, you asked me if it mattered where you sat and I said probably. Well, let's take a look at the arrangement. You and Mrs. Dietrich are sitting together on the couch, and Susanna is to the right of your wife. I suspect the fact that your wife is sitting between the two of you is no accident—any more than the fact that Kessa is sitting alone in the corner is an accident. Why are you sitting way over there in the corner, Kessa?" She shrugged her shoulders. "Do you always sit alone in corners away from the rest of your family?" Still she did not answer. "You have to answer me, Kessa."

She began to cry. "What was the question?"

"I asked if you always went off alone in corners that way. When the fighting begins, do you always withdraw and let Susanna get all of the attention?"

"I don't want that kind of attention."

"What kind of attention do you want?"

"I don't know," she mumbled through the tears.

Sherman could sense the discomfort of the rest of the family. He knew they thought he was pushing Kessa too hard. He turned to the three on the couch. "You look uncomfortable."

"Perhaps this is a bit much for Francesca,"

Grace said. "After all, she's ill and she doesn't look well."

"Mrs. Dietrich, I think everyone—including Kessa—has always thought that 'this' or any confrontation was too much for her. And that's one of the problems. You said the argument that just occurred was fairly typical." They all nodded. "And I suggested that Kessa's withdrawal to the corner might be just as typical. Moreover, I imagine you're all somewhat grateful to her for staying out of the fray."

"As a matter of fact," Harold said, "I've always felt Francesca was the most sensible of all my kids."

"That's why Susanna gets all the attention," Sherman said.

"What do you mean?" Harold was confused.

"Well, you say Francesca is the most sensible of all your kids, but Susanna's the one you devote the time and worry to."

"But why should I worry about Francesca?" Harold persisted. "She's always been a delight."

"What's the point of being a delight, Mr. Dietrich, if she's ignored for it?"

"But getting attention for being bad is wrong."

"Getting attention is right, Mr. Dietrich. Being ignored is wrong. Look at what's happened to Kessa lately. She never got so much attention in her life as she has the last several months. So what's the point of getting better if she's going to lose that attention? In fact, given the way your family works, it pays for Kessa to stay sick. If she gets better you'll only forget her and go back to worrying about Susanna and fighting with Susanna and paying attention to Susanna. Until you can learn to pay attention to Kessa for the good things as well as the bad, there's no percentage in her going back to being a good—and healthy—girl."

"Are you saying I'm responsible for my daughter's sickness?" Harold demanded.

"I'm saying that one of the factors that affects recovery in this disease is reward in terms of parental attention and affection."

"Isn't it enough of a reward for her to look and feel normal again?" Harold persisted.

Sherman looked straight at him. "Nope."

The simple answer annoyed Harold. "So you're telling me the whole thing is my fault. It's because of me that Francesca's got this crazy disease."

"Harold," Grace said softly. "Couldn't we forget about whose fault things are for a while? No one's blaming you, so why don't you stop thinking about yourself for a while and listen to what Dr. Sherman is saying."

"Mommy's right," Susanna said.

"Nobody asked your opinion," Harold shot back. "It may carry some weight at the commune, but . . ."

"You're all doing it again," Sherman interrupted, and they fell silent. "Mrs. Dietrich," he continued, "what do you want from your family?"

Grace was thoughtful for a moment. "A little more peace—and a little more fun."

"What about you, Mr. Dietrich? What do you want from your family?"

"More pleasantness. I wish we'd all be nicer to each other. And no illness. That's all. Thank heaven we're all right financially."

"And you, Susanna?" Sherman continued.

"Less fighting with Daddy. Everything's fine between Mommy and me."

All three of them seemed satisfied with their answers, but when he turned to the emaciated figure in the corner, they became uncomfortable again. Kessa felt Sherman's eyes on her but did not raise her own to his.

"What about you, Kessa? What do you want from your family?" There was no answer. "You have to answer."

The tears that had stopped so recently began again. "I don't know."

"Try to think, Kessa."

"I told you I don't know. I don't want to know. I don't want to." The words were coming faster now, as were the tears. "I don't want it and I hate it, but I need it."

"What do you mean, Kessa? What do you hate?"

"My family. I hate them, but I want them. And I hate wanting them. I hate it. I just hate it."

"Why do you hate it, Kessa?"

"I hate wanting because wanting something means you'll never get it."

Harold was surprised. "Francesca, haven't I always given you everything you've asked for?"

"What did I ever ask for? Tell me one damn thing I ever asked for."

Surprise turned to shock. Harold had never seen his younger daughter angry. "Not much, I guess."

"Not much! Nothing is more like it. I asked for nothing, and that's what I got. Gregg got admiration and Susanna got attention and I got nothing. Nothing from you and nothing from Mommy. She doesn't even like me." Kessa was sobbing now, and the words were barely audible, but the Dietrichs heard them. "She's never loved me and she never will. Mommy loves Susanna, but she doesn't give a damn about me."

Kessa looked as surprised at the last outburst as the rest of them. She covered her face with her hands and sat sobbing.

"That's not true," Grace repeated over and over. "Francesca, you know that's not true."

"Kessa," Sherman finally said when her sobs had abated, "I'm proud of you." She looked surprised, then suspicious. "For speaking up the way you just did. For saying what you felt and what you wanted."

Grace began to speak, but Sherman interrupted her. "I'm not suggesting that you don't love your daughter, Mrs. Dietrich, but the most important thing here is that Kessa feels you don't—and is asking you to. She's asking you to show your love and your attention."

Sherman turned back to Kessa. "As I said, Kessa, I'm proud of you for speaking up, for feeling your own needs and expressing them. I want you to keep on doing that. We all want you to. No one wants you to become a grouch, but we do want you to become the kind of person who will ask for—even fight for—what she wants and needs. We want you to be the kind of person who has some control over the way other people treat her."

Sherman looked at the three figures sitting together on the sofa and saw they were watching him closely. "Anorexia nervosa, an expression I'm sure you've all come to hate, is an obsession with eating and weight. An obsession is the term we give to an idea so strong, so overpowering, that it won't leave us alone. And because it won't leave us alone, we try to find ways of controlling it, so-called magical behavior that will tame it. And the magical behavior or ritual that will control it becomes in turn a compulsion. It's these compulsions that protect us from the obsession or nameless terror that can't be understood.

"There are many things," he continued, "that we don't know about obsessions and compulsions, but one thing seems fairly clear—people who are driven by them feel unable to influence the feelings and behavior of others toward them. They feel helpless in relationships, and so they are driven back into themselves and their magical rituals for controlling the way people feel about them. They live as emotional loners completely out of touch with their own needs and everyone else.

"As a family you must help Kessa to risk expressing her needs. You're going to have to encourage her to depend on you emotionally. It won't be easy, and it won't happen overnight. One week of good behavior on everybody's part isn't enough. It took a long time to establish this pattern, and it's going to take a long time to break it down. In order to help do that, I'd like to go on meeting with you as a family once a week. But for the moment, I think we've had enough."

They all looked relieved, and when her family had left and Kessa was alone with Sherman, neither of them mentioned the hour or her outburst.

"Will you stay and eat with me?" she asked.

"Sure."

The two of them left the room. "How long do I have to cart this dumb thing around?" she indicated the pole and bottle.

"For another five pounds."

"Shit."

"Yeah."

The Dietrichs talked little on the way home. Grace murmured that the doctor seemed all right, though a little hard on Francesca. Susanna said that was probably on purpose. Hal said nothing, and all three found themselves replaying the hour on the individual tapes of their own perceptions.

Susanna realized she was as concerned about the doctor's opinion of her as her father. She hadn't really been stealing the spotlight for all these years, she told herself, but still the unspoken accusation rankled.

Hal was sure a lot of what the doctor said was crazy, but he had to admit that some of it did make sense. Like the part about Francesca's getting more attention when she was sick. It was only logical that if she got more attention, she'd stay sick.

Grace, for the moment, could only hear Francesca's voice screaming the same accusation over and over: *She's never loved me and she never will! She's never loved me and she never will!*

23

A week later Myrna was up and about. Kessa and Lila were both on their beds watching television when Myrna entered carrying two lunch trays.

"Well, if it ain't the new nurse's aide," Lila quipped.

"That's not such a joke. I do almost as much work around here as they do." There was no mistaking the pride in Myrna's voice.

"If you're so strong," Lila asked, "why don't you get yourself better and go home?"

Kessa was wondering the same thing.

"I'm not ready to go home," Myrna said. "Not just yet."

"You mean you really have that much control?" Kessa was fascinated.

"Sometimes." But Myrna looked suddenly uncomfortable. "Oh, I don't know. I don't even know why I don't want to get out of here. Listen, I have to go. Why don't you come see my room this afternoon, Kessa? You've never been there."

After lunch Kessa took Myrna up on her invitation. She disliked Myrna, but she couldn't help being drawn to her—much as someone who is displeased with his appearance keeps checking it in a mirror. She found Myrna sponge-bathing one of the three other girls in the room. Kessa watched in amazement as the girl followed Myrna's orders to turn or lift an arm.

"Belinda had her appendix out," Myrna explained, "and I've been taking care of her. You want to put on your own nightgown or a hospital one?" Myrna asked the girl.

"My own," Belinda said. "It's in the drawer."

Myrna took a flowered nightie from the drawer and slipped it over Belinda's head. It was an incongruous picture, Kessa thought—the tall, frail-looking girl helping the perfectly normal-looking one.

"Thanks."

"Anytime. Listen, Kessa," Myrna said, taking her arm and beginning to help her out of the room, "I can give you a sponge bath too. The nurses say I'm as good at them as they are."

Kessa shrugged Myrna's hand from her arm. "No, thanks."

"Hey, what are you so bitchy about?"

"I'm not your patient," Kessa said. "And you're not a nurse or a doctor. You're another patient, just like me. So don't go around trying to take care of everybody."

"But I always take care of people. Here, in the last couple of hospitals, at home—especially at home. When I was eight, my mother spent a lot of time in and out of the hospital and I ran the whole house. I did the laundry, the cooking, almost everything. My wacko Aunt Harriet would come to stay while my mother was in the hospital, but I was the one who did all the work. Christ, I even took care of her. I used to mix martinis for her every night before dinner while she watched the six o'clock news. I still do a lot of the cooking. My mother works now, and she's never home in time to make dinner. Before they put me in the hospital I was cooking for the whole family, and they were all gaining weight. I was doing most of the shopping too. I bet it's tough on them now that I'm in the hospital."

"If you're such a tower of strength, how come you *are* in the hospital?"

"Some crazy doctor said I was in 'severe danger.' Severe danger, hell. I can take care of myself—and everybody else. I've never needed anybody. And it's damn lucky I haven't, because there's never been anybody there. I guess that's why I'm so terrific at taking care of myself and everybody else. I've been doing it since I was about two."

"Well, you're not going to take care of me," Kessa said, and started down the hall to her own room. She swore she'd avoid Myrna in the future.

Kessa had told herself that before, but interest in Myrna's symptoms and knowledge always overcame distaste for the girl herself. But now she found Myrna too unpleasant to tolerate. *I suppose all anorexics are like that*, Kessa thought. *And that means I'm like that too*. She confronted her image in the mirror. Suddenly she looked as ugly as her parents and all the doctors had told her she did. "You deserve to look like that," she whispered to the mirror. "You're ugly inside, and you deserve to look ugly outside."

"You talkin' to me?" Lila asked.

Kessa hadn't realized she had spoken. "No, I was just thinking out loud."

Lila returned to her magazine. Kessa was okay sometimes, but Lila didn't have much patience with her when her craziness showed. Besides, she'd be getting out soon, and the likelihood of keeping up a friendship with a crazy white girl from Central Park West was small.

Kessa watched her roommate reading the magazine. Lila probably hated her as much as she hated Myrna. Everybody hated her. Her parents, her friends, Sherman, everybody. Why not? Hadn't she just admitted to herself she was a hateful person? But the rejection was not so easy to accept.

"Hey. Lila, are you mad at me?"

"You tellin' me you'd care if I was?"

Kessa fought the impulse to lie and say she didn't give a damn what Lila thought of her. "Yeah, I'd care."

Lila looked at her in amazement. "Ever since you came in here you been actin' like the world and everyone in it includin' me is one big pain in the ass to you. You been actin' like you're better than me and smarter than me. Well, maybe you are, but I can tell you one thing. I'm smart enough to know what to do with a plate of food when they put it in front of me. And I'm smart enough not to hide food till it goes all bad and smelly and could damn near kill you."

Both girls were surprised at the outburst of anger.

"I guess I really am a bitch to live with. I guess that's why no one wants me around. Like my family not wanting me and none of my friends liking me anymore. I'm sure my mother doesn't want me home anymore, especially now that my sister's back from California."

"Boy, you're somethin'. I say one thing, and you're off on this trip feelin' so sorry for yourself you could just about die. I mean, I say you're not better than me or smarter than me, and the next thing I know you're layin' somethin' on me about your mother not wantin' you home. That ain't what I said. I didn't even say you were such a bitch to live with. I mean, you are, but hell, so am I. You hear me moanin' and cryin' and cursin' when my foot itches and I can't get to it. So what makes you think you're so much worse than me? Girl, you ain't so much better and you ain't so much worse. You're just like me and everybody else— except you're skinnier. If you got an ounce of sense left in that body of yours, you'll do somethin' about it." Lila stopped abruptly and laughed at herself. "And that's the last lecture you're gettin' from old Lila. Hell, I got my own problems to worry about. I got three flights of stairs to climb before I can even get home."

Kessa and Sherman sat on opposite sides of the desk in the small office where they regularly met, their lunch trays between them.

"Now, I don't care how much you eat, Kessa, but I'd like you to tell me when you begin to feel anxious about it."

"Okay, but I don't think it's going to be so bad this time. I've got a weird feeling, but it's a good weird feeling. And I'm glad you're eating with me."

"Well, I'm glad you can say that to me," Sherman answered. "I'm always pleased when you can talk about your feelings."

They both began to eat, and though Kessa divided the sandwich in four equal parts, there was none of the elaborate arranging of food on the plate. When she raised a forkful of cole slaw to her mouth, she did not draw back her lips to keep them from touching the utensil.

When she'd eaten half the sandwich and drunk

half a glass of milk, she stopped. "I think I'll quit now. Okay?"

"Sure," he answered through a mouthful of his own sandwich. "I'm not so hot on this stuff myself."

"Oh, I don't mind the food, but I think it's going to be a while before my stomach is stretched enough to eat a whole sandwich." She was thoughtful for a moment. "And I'm still scared of gaining too much weight. How long do you think it will take before I'm not scared of that?"

"How long do you think it'll be before you trust yourself?"

"No, I mean it, really. How long?"

"A while."

"I thought so. I wish it would go away faster. I'm terrified of gaining weight, but I really hate being this skinny."

"It sounds like you're on your way."

"But to what? That's what scares me."

"You want to know how you'll gain? What will happen to your body?"

"Yes."

He put down his fork and pushed the piece of cake away. "The first thing you'll notice is that your stomach will begin to stick out—way out. That's because it'll have food in it and look out of proportion to the rest of your body that has no fatty tissue left on it. Then you'll begin to notice new fat on your rear and a little later your thighs. Then you'll begin to gain strength in your legs so you'll be able to walk better, but I have to warn you that your ankles will be swollen for about a month and your hair will stay thin for as long as a year. But the hair over the rest of your body will begin to fall out soon. After you've replaced some weight on your lower body, your ribs and chest bones will begin to disappear. Finally you'll start to put on weight in your arms and breasts."

"Boy, am I going to look awful for a while."

"Well, it's going to be some time before you start looking healthy, but that's the shape of things to come, so to speak."

"Some shape."

"There's one other thing, Kessa. From now on —or at least until further notice—whenever you're frightened that you're gaining too much weight, call me and I'll tell you whether you are or not. I'm a better judge of your weight, so for a while we'll use my judgment instead of yours."

"What was all that crap you gave my father about each person being the best judge of his own feelings?" She reminded him of the first session with Susanna and her parents.

"We're not talking about your real feelings. We're talking about an area of your thinking where you're in trouble. And as long as you are in trouble there, I'm going to do the thinking for you."

"You know, you're the bossiest person I ever met." She was silent for a moment. "Except maybe for Myrna. You know, that other anorexic on the floor." He nodded. "She's really a pain. Maybe you could get her off my back."

"Sorry, Kessa, I only do the work for you when it comes to telling you how you really look. When it comes to your relationship with Myrna or anyone else, you've got to fight for yourself." She looked angry. "But remember, just because you're fighting for yourself, it doesn't mean you're alone. And we can talk about you and Myrna whenever you want."

"Okay, I'll do it on my own." Suddenly she smiled. "Only I don't think I'm going to tell you too much about Myrna. I think I'll let you find out for yourself. After I'm better you can start treating her. And I'm warning you, she's going to be one bitch of a patient."

Sandy laughed, but less at Kessa's joke than at his pleasure in her words. *After I am better.*

When Sherman left, Kessa, feeling warm again, promised herself she would not telephone him until her next appointment. On the way back to his office Sherman was hoping the same thing. Over the weeks, Kessa's treatment had raised personal and ethical questions for him. Should one patient be allowed to interfere with others' sessions? Should any patient take up this much of his time? It was a question his wife put to him when, staying late at the hospital to have dinner with Kessa after a Dietrich family session last week, he missed eating with his own daughters. Would they begin to think he was more interested in sick girls than in them? For a moment Sandy Sherman felt a peculiar bond with Harold Dietrich—a bond Dietrich might not recognize, but a bond nevertheless.

The phone was ringing when Sherman walked into his office. It was habit rather than a sixth sense that told him Kessa would be on the other end of the line.

"I feel so awful. I felt so good when you left here. I wasn't scared or anything, but now I'm terrified. I ate all that food, and you said my stomach was going to swell up, and oh, I don't know, I must be crazy, just crazy, but I keep swinging back and forth like this. One minute I feel one way and the next just the opposite. I don't even know who I
242

am. Or maybe I'm more than one person. Maybe I'm a split personality. Is that it? I'm a split personality?"

"Is that what you want me to say, Kessa?"

"I don't *want* you to say anything," she screamed into the phone.

"Kessa, all this turmoil you're going through is really a sign of progress."

"Progress, bullshit! I hate it! If you think this is progress you ought to try going through it yourself."

"I've told you that I know this is much harder for you than it is for me, but it *is* a sign of progress. When I first met you, you wouldn't have dared scream at me or tell me how you felt or any of this. You wouldn't talk about your feelings, and most of the time you didn't even know what they were. You were a zombie then, and what you're feeling now is all the pain and suffering you've locked up for most of your life. I know it's awful to go through it now, but I don't think there's any other way for you to get better. You're feeling awful now, Kessa, but at least you're feeling. And little by little you'll feel less terrible, until you only hurt like the rest of us—which is a lot less than the way you feel now."

"How come you know how I'm going to feel?" She wanted desperately to believe that he knew more about her than she did herself, but she was afraid.

"Haven't I been right when I told you what you were feeling before or what you were going to feel?"

"I guess so . . ."

"Would you like some good news, Kessa? I spoke to Dr. Donaldson before I left the hospital.

He said the IV can come out in four days. In four days we can walk down the hall without your sidekick. They'd do it sooner, but it takes several days for your system to get used to the reduction in nutrition. We've decided it's time to gamble on your ability to eat your way out of trouble."

Kessa felt more fear than pleasure at Sherman's words. She sat listening to him and staring at the bottle that hung next to her bed. "Are you sure it's all right?" she asked finally. "I mean I want it out, but I'm scared."

"Listen, Kessa, I'm not saying you're all better. You still look lousy, and even though you think you're eating like a horse, you're still not eating enough. But even if you're not all better, you are somewhat better, and that's why we want to give you a try. Now, remember what I said before I left the hospital. If you begin to worry about your weight, if you begin to think you're gaining too much, ask me. If you do start to gain too much weight, I promise I'll put you on a diet. But at this point you're still fifty pounds away from that possibility."

"Sometimes I know I'm not gaining weight, but I get scared anyway."

"Then you call me up and tell me you're scared, but leave out the part about getting too fat, because we know that's the fake part of your fear. Just say 'I'm scared' or 'I'm scared for my life,' which would be more accurate."

"You mean it?" she asked. "You really want me to call and say that?"

"If you feel it, Kessa—only not at two in the morning. I'm not a good shrink at that hour."

By the time Kessa hung up, she was feeling

warm again. In fact, she felt more than warm. She felt suddenly, absurdly confident. It was time, she decided, to take on Myrna. This afternoon Sherman had told her she had to work out her problems with Myrna herself, and Kessa decided now was the time to start.

She walked into Myrna's room. As Kessa waited for her to finish helping one of her roommates to the bathroom, she looked at the little kingdom Myrna had created for herself. All around her bed hung charts and pictures chronicling her illness. It was a macabre domain, but Myrna was sovereign of it.

"Come into the dayroom, Myrna," Kessa said when she had finished helping the other girl into bed. "I want to talk to you."

Myrna caught the tone of Kessa's voice and stiffened, but not in fear. She could sense a confrontation coming, but Myrna thrived on confrontations. If she wasn't helping people, she was fighting them. Anything between was impossible for Myrna. Worse than impossible—dangerous.

"Okay, kid." Myrna squared off in the dayroom. "What's your problem?"

"It isn't my problem, it's yours. Or rather, it's been mine too, but not anymore. I'm finished being sick."

"Just like that."

"No, not just like that. But it begins like that."

"Oh, sure. Listen, Kessa, I've been sick for a lot longer than you. And I've been a lot sicker. So don't try to tell me about it."

"I don't think you are sick, Myrna."

"Are you crazy?" Myrna screamed. "Ask anybody
245

on the floor. They'll tell you I'm the worst case of anorexia they ever saw."

"They'll tell me you're the biggest goddamn pain in the ass they ever saw." Kessa could not believe the words were coming from her mouth. They frightened her, but they made her feel proud and strong at the same time. "Maybe you were sick once, but you're not anymore. You're just putting on an act. And you know how I know that you're pretending? Because if you were really sick, you'd hate it. I'm really sick, and I hate it. But you love it. You think it's some kind of a game, and you're the winner."

"I don't know what you're trying to prove anyway." Myrna's tone was petulant now. She could put up a good fight when she understood the terrain, but this battlefield was in a foreign country.

Suddenly Kessa felt relieved. When she spoke, her voice was much calmer. "I'm not trying to prove anything. I don't have to anymore. I don't have to prove it to you because I know it myself. It stinks to be sick. I don't give a damn if you know it or admit it, because I know it now. It stinks to be sick, so I'm going to get better and get out of this place. I'm going to be a normal person."

"Anorexics never get better. Ask any of the doctors or nurses. You may get out of here for a while, but you'll never get better."

Kessa remembered Sherman's reassurances. "Wanna bet?" she tossed over her shoulder as she left the room.

Myrna, however, did not take the defeat easily. That night she cornered Kessa in the corridor. "So you're going to get better, huh? What a laugh. I've been watching you for the past ten minutes, racing up and down this hall like some goddamn marathon runner. What are you doing now if you're not trying to burn up calories? You're never going to get better that way, smart-ass." Myrna's shriveled face contorted in a cruel grin.

Without saying a word Kessa turned and went back to her room. She lay flat on her back and stared up at the ceiling, but she could not regulate her breathing. She felt as if someone were trying to strangle her. *I'm scared*, she thought. *I'm scared for my life*. She rolled on her side and began to dial the familiar number. "Sandy . . .," she began.

As soon as Sherman hung up the phone, it rang again. "Sandy, Bernie Donaldson here. You want me to soft soap you or give it to you straight?"

"I'm crazy about your bedside manner, Bernie. Okay, give it to me straight."

"How would you like to take on another anorexic? You've seen her on the floor. Myrna Link. And before you answer, I think I ought to tell you she's been in and out of hospitals and psychiatrists' offices for more than three years. It's a hard-core case."

"You mean one that can't be helped, only maintained?"

"Boy, you never give up, do you? Okay, I'm eating my words. I think between us we can help her. At least, I'd like to give it a try."

"That means I'll be treating four anorexics at the same time."

"Listen, Sandy, I didn't call to listen to your problems. You're the shrink."

"It also means two of my patients will know each other."

247

"When you finish debating the professional ethics of the problem you can give me an answer."

Sherman thought for a moment. I must be crazy, he told himself. "Okay, we'll take her on."

24

When Sherman entered Kessa's room, she was sitting on her bed writing. His eyes ran down her with professional interest. The ankles were still swollen, but otherwise she was looking better than he had ever seen her. And she'd been off the hyperal for a month now.

"Getting an early start on next year's homework?"

"I'm writing a letter. To my brother Gregg." Sherman raised his eyebrows. "To tell him what a shit I think he is."

Sandy laughed. "I think that's terrific. It'll probably be good for both of you."

"Well, I don't know if it's going to do Gregg any good, but it feels great to me. I told him he was a louse for not coming to visit me even once." She looked at Sherman thoughtfully. "If you had a sister in the hospital, you'd get away for a weekend to visit her, wouldn't you?"

"I'd sure try to, Kessa. And what's more important, if I was in the hospital and my sister didn't bother to visit me, I'd be mad as hell."

"That's exactly what I am, and I'm telling Gregg."

"Good for you! Now, I know Dr. Donaldson and I made the right decision."

He could see in Kessa's face that she knew what was coming and was both happy and frightened.

"You've been off the hyperal for a month, been here in the hospital for almost three. You weigh eighty-five, which is what we agreed on. I think it's time for you to go home, Kessa."

"Why? I mean, Lila's still here. Why do I have to go?"

"Kessa." Sandy shook his head.

"Well, I still get scared sometimes. I mean, I want to go home, but there have been times in the last month, even the last week, when I still felt scared. Of eating and everything else."

"I know that, Kessa, but you're not as scared as you used to be, and you're not scared as much of the time, are you?"

"I guess not." She was silent for a moment remembering the horrors and the panic of last spring. Every time she pictured her room, she saw herself lying on her bed examining her newly emerging bones. When she thought of the bathroom at the end of the hall, the whole complement of rituals came back to her. She saw herself at the dinner table fighting with her father and mother.

"But I'm not sure how I'm going to feel once I'm home."

"I'll tell you how you're going to feel, Kessa." It was, of course, the answer she was hoping for. "For a while you probably won't feel as comfortable as you've come to feel here. You're going to be scared at first. You may even lose a few pounds." She looked alarmed. "But that doesn't mean you're going to lose everything you've gained here—and I don't mean just weight. You're going to be returning to a setting and a situation that helped you get sick in the first place, so naturally some aspects of it are going to frighten you. And you're going to have to fight them and the fear. But only for a while. After that I'm convinced you'll go on getting better as you have here."

"Do you think I'll ever get completely better?"

For the hundredth time Sherman remembered that early talk with Donaldson, and suddenly there was no doubt in his mind.

"I know you will, Kessa. And I haven't been wrong so far, have I?"

"Well, you haven't been wrong, but now I think you're lying to me."

"What do you mean?"

"If I always have to ask you for the answers, then I'm never going to get really better. I'll never be like everybody else if I'm so dependent on you."

"We've been through this before," Sherman reminded her gently. "As soon as we've got your dependence together, then we'll begin to work on your independence. I didn't say you were going to be all better tomorrow, Kessa, but I did say you're going to be all better in time."

"Will I still see you twice a week?" she asked.

"Yup. Now if that's all clear, you can finish your letter and begin getting your act together. Tomorrow's moving day. They want this bed for someone who's sick."

He was almost out the door when she called to him. "Sandy?"

"Yes."

"Will I still be able to call you?"

Sherman walked back to where she sat and ruffled the hair that was still thin. "You'll be able to call me whenever you want, Kessa. You know why?"

She smiled, knowing the answer he wanted her to give. "Because I don't have to be sick to get attention?"

"Because you don't have to be sick to get attention."

25

On the day Kessa was scheduled to leave the hospital, Harold Dietrich did not go to his office.

"You didn't have to take the day off," Grace told him. Nevertheless she was glad he had.

"I did have to take the day off," Harold said. "If I took time off to put her in the hospital, I can damn well take time off to bring her home."

"Hurrah for Daddy," Susanna said.

Harold shot her a look, but he could find sarcasm neither in her face nor in her voice.

"You're right, Hal," Grace said. "You did have to take the day off. Bringing Francesca home from the hospital is at least as important as taking her there. Now," Grace added as she started for the door, "if we can all just remember that."

Kessa stood at the window of the dayroom staring out at the crazy-quilt of apartment houses, wondering about all the people living alone and separate in all the little apartments. Behind her she heard Lila and two other girls starting a game of Monopoly. Kessa looked at her watch. Her parents wouldn't be here for at least another hour. She walked to where the three girls sat over the Monopoly board.

"Hey, can I join?"

More Helpful Reading from
WARNER BOOKS